Why I Am a Christian
Volume 2

Kent Philpott

EVP
Earthen Vessel Publishing

Why I Am a Christian
Volume 2

All rights reserved
Copyright © 2014 by Kent A. Philpott

Published 2014 by
Earthen Vessel Publishing
San Rafael, CA 94903
www.evpbooks.com

Cover and Book Design by
Katie L. C. Philpott

ISBN: 978-0-9898041-5-8 (print version)

ISBN: 978-0-9898041-6-5 (ebook version)

No part of this publication may be reproduced, stored in a retrieval system, or transmitted in any form or by any means, electronic or mechanical, including photocopying, recording, or by any information retrieval system, without the written permission of the author or publisher, except by a reviewer who wishes to quote brief passages in connection with a review written for inclusion in a magazine, newspaper, internet site, or broadcast.

All Scripture quotations, unless otherwise indicated, are taken from the Holy Bible, English Standard Version® (ESV®), copyright © 2001 by Crossway Bibles, a publishing ministry of Good News Publishers. Used by permission. All rights reserved.

Contents

Preface	5
Part One	7
Why I Am a Christian	8
Legalistic Grace	32
The Big Gamble	36
Bill's Pain	39
Is Sin a Disease?	42
Lyman Beecher: How He Died	47
Taking Away Hope	50
What is Happening to Hell?	56
It Amazes Me	63
The Real Reason	67
Soul Confusion	70
"You're a Fundamentalist, aren't you?"	78
What Can the Unconverted Do?	84
I Don't Care Anymore!	87
How It Works	90
How We Know We Are Christians	95

Part Two	104
If It's Organized Religion, It Must Be Bad	105
Strikes and Outs	110
We Are Hypocrites, You Know	117
Feeling the Spirit?	121
Christian Moralistic Therapeutic Deism	128
Christian Mystics	133
Discouraged, Anyone?	138
Homophobia and Heterophobia	141
Mindfulness: Another View	151
Got an App?	154
God's Will is Simple and Clear	157
Something Good about Hell	161
The Anointing. The Anointing. The Anointing.	165
The Contract	174
Adam and Eve in the History of Salvation	177
The Key to Reformed Theology	185
Male/Female: The Nature of God	197
Walking, Talking, and Eating with Jesus	200

Preface

In 2002 Evangelical Press published *Why I am a Christian*. Now in 2014 Earthen Vessel Publishing is presenting a new version of the book, with some re-writing plus additional new essays.

Part One is the original *Why I am a Christian*, with the exception of chapter two. The original chapter two, "A death blow to Christianity" is entirely out-dated, so it did not make the cut. In its place is one of my favorite essays and one that attracted a lot of attention, not all of it uplifting.

Part Two consists of eighteen new essays written over the past eight years, and some are very recent.

Each essay fits generally with the overall theme of the book, which is set forth in the lead essay, "Why I am a Christian." The purpose of this new publication is to speak to those who are not yet Christian but are thinking about it. Also, it is for those who have begun following Jesus and are curious about any number of issues, which I am hoping may be addressed in one or another of the essays.

Kent Philpott
August, 2014

Part One

Sixteen Essays

One

Why I Am a Christian

Given all the barriers and obstacles that stood in my way, I am surprised I became a Christian at all. Immediately prior to my conversion, I was in jeopardy of walking away without Christ forever.

After fifty years as a Christian and forty-five years as a minister of the gospel, I have discovered a number of obstacles, hindrances, barriers, or scandals that may keep a person from becoming a Christian. What these obstacles are and how they may be overcome is the subject of this chapter. To put it another way, "Why am I a Christian?"

The exclusiveness of Jesus

The idea of Jesus being the only Savior was, to my mind, an expression of ignorance and arrogance. To many non-believers, the idea that Jesus is God seems absurd. To their thinking, the claim that Jesus is the exclusive means to the Creator of the entire universe appears puerile and simplistic.

At the time of my conversion, my concept of God was confused. I had a vague notion that there might be a God, but admitting that there is a particular God who had become a man and had acted to bring a rebellious people to himself was beyond the scope of my understanding. And suggesting that this God was the only true God offended the liberal sensitivities I had gained through the course of my college education.

Our general populace and some liberal Christians have abandoned the concept of the exclusiveness of Jesus. Inclusiveness, diversity, political correctness, relativism – these are powerful ideas that have persuaded many to deny the exclusive claims of the Bible about Christ. This departure from historic Christian doctrine is rather commonplace now. However, many Christians do adhere to Scripture, and thus the preeminence of Christ survives. If, at the time of my pre-conversion crisis, I had encountered someone championing the cause of liberal Christianity, I may well have been persuaded by such reasoning or at least would have become more confused than I already was. Instead, I heard a preacher who stuck to the Book and would not compromise one word.

Still, the notion that God should love only Christians violates a certain sense of fairness. What about those in third world countries who do not know anything about Jesus? What about them? What kind of a God is this anyway? What about those who cannot find their way to the narrow path – are they condemned forever to a devil's hell? Particularly heartbreaking is the idea that the innocents of the world – children and those raised in deplorable and hopeless conditions who never even hear of Jesus – will be lost forever. For me, this is perhaps the most troubling doctrinal position of all, even though I am in my fifth decade as a Christian. It will probably trouble me all my life. There are no words I can think of to settle my mind about it. Yet I know the God and Father of my Lord Jesus Christ is loving and merciful beyond description. There is abundant testimony in the Bible that God loves everyone. Of this I am sure. While I will leave the hard questions for him to answer in his way and in his time, even such tough issues as these do not have the power to distort or negate the truth of Jesus and his cross.

This exclusiveness barrier was not removed by logic, revelation, or careful analysis. All these years later, I have more easily, though not completely, reconciled the difficulty of the narrow path to Jesus. I also considered that the creator God, with a single focused purpose and plan, as would be reasonable, might well provide to all his creation the same way to be reconciled to him. Why have a host of different plans? It would only serve to confuse everyone. A God who changed constantly would not be reliable. A God who treated people differently might be a confused God.

Consider that the gods of the world's religions are quite different from one another, to the point of being mutually exclusive. This is not a treatise on world religions, but the plain fact is, they are not the same, despite the sophistry of the masses that claims, "All paths lead to God." I have read the basics of the world's religions, and their belief systems contradict one another, which is especially true for Hinduism, Buddhism, Islam, and Christianity. Using a popular means of comparing things, it is not apples and apples. It is not even like comparing two kinds of fruit, but more like fruit and rocks, and even this comparison does not adequately express the tremendous differences.

There is no question that the "Jesus only" barrier is enough to keep someone from Christ. It nearly kept me from him.

Judgment and hell

Most non-believers know that Christians claim their God knows all things and is all-powerful. Why, they ask, would such a God create people who have numerous personal flaws that make them prone to break his laws and then predestine them to spend eternity in hell? Such a God seems monstrously capricious and cruel.

What troubled me was the question, "How could a loving God condemn one of his creatures to a horrible place forever?" This was the nature of the barrier.

The preacher presented it loud and clear – judgment and hell awaited all who did not trust in Jesus. It was with this pronouncement that a fire and brimstone Baptist preacher confronted me. The liberal preachers, heavy on love and soft on wrath, did not convince me, although I am not sure why not. I suppose I already believed what they taught: be sincere and loving, sit in church and pray, give to those less fortunate, and do good works. That was their whole message. But in the back of my mind I wondered. If these universal salvation preachers were right, then I had nothing to worry about. However, if they were wrong, I was in trouble. Not that I was a terribly awful person, but I was definitely not holy and without sin, and I had no plans to change. I thought that the few sins I committed to supposedly help me cope with the troubles of life were innocent enough. There were just a few major ones continuing from my youth, and I thought I could work on them somehow.

Yet the thundering from the pulpit made God sound awful to me. I thought it would have been wiser for the pastor to delete those points on judgment and hell and create, in today's jargon, a more "user friendly" church. This was not good psychology, and I wondered if the preacher even knew what he was doing. Though he persisted in it, I must admit that he did not mention it much, maybe once or twice; but I could not get it out of my mind.

I resisted the thought that I could be frightened into becoming a Christian and having to change my ways. If I had to go to hell, I thought at least I would not be alone. If that was my due, then so be it. Getting me all worked up about hell would not do the trick.

But then I kept remembering something the preacher said. Would Jesus really say to human beings, "Depart from me, I never knew you"? The preacher said he would. Would the torment be so terrible that a condemned person would plead for even a drop of water? And would it mean being shut up forever with the demons and the devil? The preacher said it would, because that was what the Bible taught. I never did resolve the problem of judgment and hell before my conversion, and it still is quite disturbing to me.

I have, however, come to believe those doctrines, because I see them throughout the Scriptures, and they are entirely logical. God made a perfect world and created humans in his own image. They then rebelled against him and thus lost the fellowship they had with him. Their sin separated them or, more precisely, severed the relationship between them and their God. From then on, death means that we humans cannot be with God where he dwells in heaven. We cannot be in his holy presence with our sin against us. And because everyone will be raised eternally, those of us separated from God by our sin will have to spend it elsewhere – in a place called hell. This hell, created as an everlasting abode for the devil and demons, will be the final home of the unrighteous. This is the sentence to be handed down at the final judgment of God.

There it is: judgment and hell. What a barrier! We, with our limited understanding, are offended by such an idea. It is an obstacle so high, that no one can get over it or around it, no matter how hard one tries.

The problem of grace

How can grace be a problem? Grace – the love, mercy, and forgiveness of God given freely to those who do not deserve it – is indeed a wonderful gift.

Grace is God electing us to salvation. Since we have no

ability to come to him on our own, he comes to us. Actually, the Father draws us to his Son. And when he does, we hear (not to be taken in a literal sense) the voice of Jesus calling out to us; we hear him knocking, and we arise and open that door. He comes in and dwells with us, because it is his will and desire to do so.

Grace is a barrier, because it implies that we cannot control our own destiny. This is the heart of it. Inasmuch as grace is a gift from God that we cannot earn, it follows that we are powerless to make ourselves acceptable to God. We cannot forgive our own sin; no matter what we do, we cannot make ourselves righteous.

In my self-righteousness and pride I proclaimed, "I am a good person, as good as or better than anyone else, and what's more, I am a spiritual and compassionate person." The biblical doctrine of grace denotes that all of these fine qualities are of no value whatsoever when it comes to being right before God. This made me angry.

The Scriptures declare, "So then it depends not on human will or exertion, but on God, who has mercy" (Romans 9:16). Since grace is offensive to us, we are tempted to invent a religion by which we can earn our own way. This is the foundation of all religions except biblical Christianity. The opposite of grace expresses itself like this: work hard, study hard, be sincere, love others, serve those in need, attain to a loving and compassionate consciousness, and so on, all done by our own effort. We may go so far as to mouth the old adage, "God helps those who help themselves." But in our pride we reject grace, for grace is really God giving us what we cannot earn. We stubbornly refuse grace and say, "Away with it, I will do it myself. I am man, I am woman, I am my own person."

We even proudly proclaim, "I am my own god and in control of my own destiny." Tell me I am the master of my fate, and I will bow down and worship before this altar and this god created in my image. Declare that I am without sin or that there is no such thing as sin, and I will embrace such ideas enthusiastically. But don't tell me I am a sinner, dead and lost and condemned, or I might rise up in a rare moment of intolerance and accuse you of being narrow and bigoted or worse.

The self-willed person cannot extinguish the offensive nature of grace. This barrier will not be removed, for if grace is removed, there can be no forgiveness. Jesus has done all that is necessary, all that can ever be done for my salvation. Now he stands offering it to me freely. This is grace. When I did not love him, he loved me. When I despised and rejected him, he longed to be my Savior. When I heaped abuse upon him, he prayed that I might be forgiven. This is grace.

Grace challenges most of my life experience, because I have been taught to expect punishment or rewards depending on my behavior. But grace contradicts this universal experience. Outside of the grace of Jesus we know only reward or punishment, perhaps the concept of karma, and the best we can hope for is an even break. But we cannot break even; in reality we will only experience repeated failure, guilt, and despair.

What a barrier – without Jesus we can do nothing. Yet when we see this great and liberating truth, we can experience grace, and the obstacle will be overcome.

The devil and the demons

What proof is there of a devil? There is none that would stand up to scientific scrutiny, even though those who are committed to the reality of paranormal experiences may advance certain evidence.

The worlds' religions are full of stories of demons and devils. Most may be fanciful and mythical, but the fact remains that people on earth believe and have believed in the demonic from the beginning. There are probably more religious ceremonies, litanies, and rituals designed to ward off or placate evil spirits than any other religious activity taking place on a day by day basis. However, this alone proves nothing.

The Bible speaks of a literal devil named Satan. It also speaks of demons. In short, Satan was a ruling angel who rebelled against God at some time in the distant past, and the demons are those angels who sided with him in that rebellion. Those beings then allied themselves against the one supreme Deity and all that this Creator God made – especially those who were created in his own image, humans. Yet, this biblical "proof" does not measure up to scientific examination either. The existence of Satan and demons is a matter of faith. Though some claim direct experience with the devil, as I do myself, yet it is subjective in nature and not the kind of proof that would stand up to empirical scientific inquiry.

Counter arguments for the devil's existence, though compelling, prove nothing either. For the sake of fairness, I will point out some of the more potent arguments against the reality of demonic forces. Firstly, if God knows everything, then why didn't he know that some of his angels would rebel and refrain from creating the rebellious ones? Secondly, if God has complete power to do anything, then why didn't he destroy the rebellious angels before they could harm people? Thirdly, if Satan and the demons will be cast into hell sometime in the future, then why doesn't God do away with them right now? Fourthly, if God created soon-to-be-fallen angels, then why didn't he make them interested in tadpoles, so that people would be left in peace? Fifthly, if God created angels who would fall, then why doesn't he admit his mistake? Sixthly, if it is not a mistake, then God must not love his people all that much.

A thorough examination of the Bible would satisfy us on

some of these points, but even armed with scriptural explanations, the existence of the demonic would still be a matter of faith. Furthermore, several of the counter arguments bring up the issue of theodicy, or the justification of a good God in the face of evil, a subject long and futilely debated over the millennia.

So then, we have the problem of how preposterous the existence of the devil may seem. If, in fact, there is a devil, then that should also lead us to wonder what influence such a crafty, subtle, and powerful being (as the Bible depicts Satan) has upon us. Prior to my conversion, I was unaware of any influence the devil might have had on me. Yet, when I ask myself where all my antagonism against Christianity, the Bible, church, and Christians sprang from, I also wonder if it all originated with me alone? I think that is possible, but based on what I know now, I think the devil must bear at least some of the responsibility.

I haven't figured out why evil exists or why a loving God would allow evil to exist in the first place. I doubt I ever will. While I have some idea of how to resolve these issues tucked away in a systematic theological model in the back of my mind, it is virtually impossible for me to recapitulate it to anyone. If pressed, I would say that Jesus himself believed in the existence of both Satan and demons. This is the most telling point for me, inasmuch as Jesus has ultimate integrity for me. He is Truth himself, and I have learned I can trust him.

Regarding the other point, given the reality of the demonic: How might the demonic influence a human being? Paul wrote, "The god of this age has blinded the minds of the unbelievers, to keep them from seeing the light of the gospel of the glory of Christ, who is the image of God" (2 Corinthians 4:4). Satan, the god of this age, blinds minds so that people either cannot perceive Jesus at all or fail to understand his message. Usually it is the latter.

In my case I did not understand that Jesus was the Son of God, the Savior. That he was a historical figure who actually lived on earth was not a problem for me. I believed Jesus was the founder of a religion and considered him to be a great teacher, but I never believed he was the Savior who took my sin upon himself on the cross and who later rose from the dead.

When Jesus died upon the cross, he won the great victory over the devil. In fact, Jesus completely defeated Satan and will finally put Satan away forever into hell when he returns at the end of the age. Although Satan has power to blind the minds of non-believers, he does not have ultimate power. The Father calls people to his Son Jesus according to his own will. The apostle John put it this way: "The reason the Son of God appeared was to destroy the works of the devil" (1 John 3:8).

Perhaps the most vivid example of Jesus' triumph over Satan is the story of the man dwelling in the tombs in a region known as the Gerasenes. He had a legion, meaning many, many, demons living in him This outcast had been reduced to the most horrible existence and was beyond the help of anyone, but when he met Jesus the demons that had tormented and demented him were cast into a herd of pigs. Finally in his right mind, he became an evangelist to his countrymen (see Luke 8:26-39). This is perfectly in tune with what Jesus said he would do. "The thief comes only to steal and kill and destroy; I have come that they may have life, and have it abundantly" (John 10:10).

"Blessed is the one who takes no offence at me." These words of Jesus are the reason for this book. Piled up four deep now, the hindrances might seem insurmountable, but they are nothing but straw. There is no real offence in Jesus.

The scandalous history of the church

There are two churches today, and it has been like this from the beginning. One church is visible – the organization, the institution – and it is far from perfect, sometimes very far from anything resembling perfect. The other is the true Church, probably tiny in proportion to the visible church, and it is made up of all those who are genuine, born-again Christians. This true Church may be intermingled with the institutional church, while parts of the true Church may exist outside of the visible church altogether.

"For the word of the cross is folly to those who are perishing, but to us who are being saved it is the power of God" (1 Corinthians 1:18). Because of this truth, there has been an effort on the part of church leaders, almost right from the beginning and throughout the course of church history, to avoid the scandal of the cross. Since the idea of the cross is foolishness to so many, there is a desire to replace it with ideas more readily acceptable to worldly people. It might be said that the true Church consists of those who are born again of the Spirit and adhere to and preach the message of the cross where Jesus, God in the flesh, died for our sin. This Church cannot be identified with any one group, denomination, theological model, or leader.

The visible church (es), with all their various names, doctrines, and leaders, developed political power, accumulated wealth, and worst of all, devised magical means whereby forgiveness and salvation were dispensed. They came to represent what all the world thought was biblical Christianity, but it was not.

Therefore, there are two histories of the church, and most of us are not able to easily distinguish between them. In his book, Concerning Scandals, John Calvin wrote that the church "never shines with that splendor which would enable the minds of men to recognize the Kingdom of God." Even the true Church, the Church that clings to the cross of Jesus, is itself not pure and free from error, because it is composed of sinners not completed, even darkened in their understanding. It is no surprise that both churches and everything associated with them are prone to scandal.

The history of the early church, as found in the New Testament Book of Acts, reveals a less than perfect collection of believers. Acts 5 records members of the church lying to the apostles about money. Acts 6 contains details of trouble over the unequal distribution of food to certain widows, and the apostles themselves were implicated. In Acts 15 there is the account of a debate about the doctrine of salvation. Of the seven churches in Asia (see the opening chapters of Revelation) only one church escaped Jesus' criticism altogether. There is more, but the point is that the church is not pictured as perfect in its most important and public document, the Bible. The early church had its problems, and Paul in particular wrote letters to correct several aspects of the doctrines and behaviors of various congregations. Curiously, the church's internal difficulties did not provoke any would-be censors. The Bible records it that way, because that is what happened.

It should therefore be understood that what history might call the church was (and is) not necessarily the elect Church of God at all, but only a worldly institution that contains some true believers. We think of the crusades, the witch trials of Salem, the Inquisition, forced conversions of Jews, and a thousand other atrocities, and we wonder whether this all should be laid at the door of the church? The institutional church, or some form of it, is responsible for these and other horrible events, although even God's elect Church is composed of saints who are nonetheless sinners. Therefore, history will record one grievous episode after the other, but I believe there is less true scandal than most people might imagine.

One reason the church's history is full of scandal is that the enemy of God, Satan, and those who belong to that dark kingdom fight a dirty and horrific war against all those who trust in Jesus. Consider the following: Jesus warned that false Christians and prophets would appear and perform great signs and wonders, so that even the true Christians might be deceived (see Matthew 24:24). Paul wrote something similar: "Now the Spirit expressly says that in later times some will depart from the faith by devoting themselves to deceitful spirits and teachings of demons" (1 Timothy 4:1). In addition, Paul warned the Corinthian church about false teachers operating in the midst of the church itself: "For such men are false apostles, deceitful workmen, disguising themselves as apostles of Christ" (2 Corinthians 11:13). In the organized church there will be false apostles empowered by Satan himself. Is it any wonder that the history of such a church is full of scandal?

Remember, the good and bad elements of the church are so intermingled that it is often impossible to tell the difference. In a parable, Jesus warned against trying to make distinctions. His warning is so pertinent to a proper understanding of the mixed nature of the church, I quote its entirety here:

> "The kingdom of heaven may be compared to a man who sowed good seed in his field, but while his men were sleeping, his enemy came and sowed weeds among the wheat and went away. So when the plants came up and bore grain, then the weeds appeared also. The servants of the master of the house came to him and said, 'Master, did you not sow good seed in your field? How then does it have weeds?' He said to them, 'An enemy has done this.' So the servants

said to him, 'Then do you want us to go and gather them?' But he said, 'No, lest in gathering the weeds you root up the wheat along with them. Let both grow together until the harvest, and at harvest time I will tell the reapers, Gather the weeds first and bind them in bundles to be burned, but gather the wheat into my barn'" (Matthew 13:24-30).

Like any diabolic and clever opponent, Satan's tactic is to attack the message by attacking the messenger. In the broadest sense, the church is that messenger, and so the archenemy must make every attempt to besmirch it. This must be understood, in order to have an accurate understanding of church history.

There is a true Church, the Church elect and called by God; and he alone knows who are his. This Church is perfect, because it is the Body of Christ. And Christ is in the midst of his church, the Church Triumphant. This Church is gathered to worship, honor, and serve the God and Father of our Lord Jesus Christ. To this Church Jesus promised that the gates of hell would not prevail against it. The history of the church demonstrates the truth of Jesus' statement, despite the fact that from those hellish gates every foul and scandalous evil will emerge.

The hypocrisy of believers

All Christians are hypocrites, and because of this, non-believers will be tempted to reject Jesus.

Webster's New Universal Unabridged Dictionary defines "hypocrite" as "a person who pretends to have virtues, moral and religious beliefs, principles, etc., that he or she does not actually possess, especially a person whose actions belie stated beliefs" (1996 edition). I have to admit to falling into the category of a hypocrite on the basis of this definition.

Prior to my conversion I knew that Christians were hypocrites; in fact, I used it as an excuse to reject Christian claims. I heard of one girl who was a Christian and attended church but was notoriously promiscuous. Some of my friends dated her, and it made me particularly angry that she would not go out with me. Whether she was a real Christian I cannot say, but the whole situation served to prejudice me against Christianity.

My perception, although I am not sure where it came from, was that Christians had to be perfect. I reasoned that if you are a Christian, then you have to be perfectly loving and ethical. And if not, then, "Ah-ha, see! You are a fake and a liar, and your Christianity is bogus, too." This is how I saw things, and it suited my rebellion perfectly.

There is no question that I am a hypocrite, too. It is not my intention to be one, but I find that I am. A hypocrite is someone who professes to be something and is not. I profess to be perfect in Christ, but I am far less than that. There is a sense, however, in which I am perfect, because God sees me as perfect since I was placed into Christ at the moment of my conversion. I am still a sinner, not perfect, and I will remain so until the very moment of my death.

Christians do the strangest things, as I know from my experience as a pastor for several decades. Even the best of us fall short of the ideal, because the standard is so very high – Jesus himself. When his life is examined, it is clear that he was no hypocrite. No, he is the Lamb of God without blemish; though tempted to sin in every way that we are, he is without sin of any kind. Jesus, the sinless one, said that we are to be perfect as the Father in heaven is perfect, and therein lays the problem.

The "perfect yet sinner" paradox is true of all Christians, and it is quite biblical. Paul confessed that the things he did not want to do he did, and conversely, the things he wanted to do, he did not do (Romans 7:15-20). What a scandal this has produced. If anyone is looking for a reason to castigate Christianity, he will not have to look far. I should point out that a careful examination of Paul's life would not have revealed him to be some kind of wild sinner indulging the flesh at every opportunity. In fact, it might have taken a close examination to find anything amiss at all. But Paul knew the high calling he had in Christ, and when he was honest with himself, he had to admit that he did not always act in accordance with his calling.

In the pages of the New Testament there are stories of some notable hypocrites. Peter comes immediately to mind. He was the first of the apostles to confess that Jesus was the Messiah. Then, before very long, he denied Jesus three times. There were also the two zealous disciples in the early Jerusalem church, Ananias and his wife Sapphira, who turned out to be cheats and liars (Acts 5:1-5). One of Paul's companions, a missionary by the name of Demas, completely abandoned Paul, the gospel, and Christ; he rebelled and returned to a sinful life (see 2 Timothy 4:9-10). Consider, however, that the biblical writers made no attempt to hide or clean up the historical record. They let it stand as it was. Hypocrisy was expected, because the integrity and truth of Christianity does not reside with individual Christians, but depends exclusively on Jesus alone, the solid foundation and ground of it all.

Christians are bound to appear as hypocrites. We have always known this. Some of the greatest heroes in the history of the post-apostolic church have been inconsistent, although inconsistent is far too innocuous a term to describe some of the antics of the saints. Acknowledging this in Concerning Scandals, John Calvin wrote, "It is wrong for us to measure the eternal truth of God by the changing inconstancy of men" (p. 78). Then in the same place, he continued, "Will the treacherous desertion of certain individuals overthrow our faith?" Of course he expects the answer to be a resounding, No!

Early in my Christian life I could not help but notice that I did not give up sinning even though I wanted to. At one point I thought I should not be spending any time with those "good people" down at the church. It was not enough that no one knew what a rascal I was; I knew it, and so I thought that Christianity must not be working. Yet I hung on, refused to give up, and finally realized that everyone was just the same as me.

As time went on, I believed I was making a little progress. I noticed that, although some of my sin seemed to stop, that I would discover or even develop new sins. This has been the case the entire time I have been a Christian. I am never going to get away from the fact that I am a hypocrite. Hopefully, non-believers will not use my failures and inconsistencies to reject the gospel. I have decided that I do not want to hide from people in order to keep my sin private. No, I want to live an honest and open life. So, I intend to grow up into the stature of the fullness of Christ, and even when someone gets to know me well, they will not be caused to stumble by what they see.

Christians are bound to be seen as hypocrites by those who want to rebel against God. All they have to do is watch one of us for a while, and they will soon find some indiscretion, real or imagined, and that will be enough to turn them from Christ. This barrier can only be overcome by the Holy Spirit of God working to convert a sinner.

The trouble with the Bible

How I despised the Bible! One day I caught my wife reading it, and in anger I took it from her hands, threw it across the room, and ordered her never to bring a Bible into our apartment again.

Later, I had to read portions of the Bible for a term paper for a college philosophy of religion course. Failing to understand anything about it, I became so frustrated that I vowed never to touch a Bible again.

This is the trouble with the Bible – it is incomprehensible to those who do not have the Spirit of God. Paul put it this way: "The natural person does not accept the things of the Spirit of God, for they are folly to him, and he is not able to understand them, because they are spiritually discerned" (1 Corinthians 2:14). I can personally verify the truth of this verse, and have observed it in hundreds of people over the years. Many people who had consistently avoided the Bible developed a thirst for it after their conversion, and that desire for it never went away.

In our unconverted state we rebel against the Bible and what it teaches. This rebellion may take a passive or aggressive form. My own was aggressive, illustrated by my throwing a Bible across the room. Most people's rebellion takes a passive form – they simply ignore it. Even many well-educated people do this, despite the fact that the Bible is the most influential book ever published in our culture. Whether one agrees with it or not, more copies of it are printed and sold each year than any other book. The Bible, with its wonderful and timeless stories, flowing language, and flawless grammar, transcending all other books, is regularly ignored by the literati.

Why is this so? The reason has already been expressed – the Bible is a spiritual book, and unless the Spirit of God reveals its truth, it will remain unintelligible. Furthermore, the Bible does not flatter the human spirit. The Bible calls sin sin, and it does so in no uncertain terms. It also presents a God to whom every person is responsible, since he will judge the living and the dead according to their faith in his Son,

Jesus the Christ. The Bible is rejected because of its message. We react against the Bible, because we have broken God's laws and have become corrupt.

One of the difficulties with the Bible is that it is written by real people, and their personalities and peculiar literary styles are apparent. Therefore, it does not appear to be a spiritual book at all. The Bible is the history of God, or stories about God and his people, from the creation to the prophecies about the end of the universe, told by flawed and imperfect people, although under the inspiration of the Holy Spirit. The ancient people of God pieced it together over a very long period of time. It is unlike any other religious or spiritual document in existence.

I cannot prove that the Bible is the true word of God, but given enough space, I could certainly make a strong case for it. There is plenty of solid evidence that points towards that conclusion. I could write at length of prophecies fulfilled; or of forty authors over a 1500-year span, in three languages and even more cultures, from Moses to John of the Revelation, weaving the same, seamless cloth; or of countless numbers of people over the course of thousands of years whose lives have been redeemed, transformed, and rescued through the Book's direct influence; or of the great nations and institutions whose foundation is the great Book. But none of it would be enough to prove the inspiration of the Bible objectively. It is a matter of subjective and collective faith, and when proven in this way, that proof is stronger than anything objective or empirical could ever be.

For me, the one great proof for the authenticity of the Bible is that Jesus believed the Old Testament to be the very word of God. Moreover, the New Testament is the record of Jesus, his life and ministry. Therefore, Jesus is the reason for my confidence in it all.

I trust Jesus. It is that simple. Having examined his life by reading the Gospels a hundred times or more, I find Jesus to be the very definition of integrity. In him, there is no inconsistency, no pride or selfishness, no hint of sin, vainglory, or deceit. In all his ways and words he is pure and holy. No one has ever been able to prove against him any wrongdoing. I trust the Scriptures, because I trust Jesus.

Even this argument, however, will not persuade the skeptic. The Bible will always be troublesome until the Author reveals himself to the reader.

Christian fluff

As a teenager in Los Angeles, my friends and I would spy the neon sign, "Jesus Saves," in large, garish, yellow and red letters atop a building, and we would ask, "What does Jesus save?" and the answer would be, "Green Stamps."

You have to be my age or older to fully appreciate this exchange, but we saw that sign as part of the Christian fluff of the time. Today, such jingoism seems to be the signature of "devout" Christians: T-shirts, baseball caps, signs in novelty shops, tattoos on Christians' bodies – seemingly endless trite and worn-out statements that are somehow taken to be expressions of Christian piety. Fluffy, corny, mindless caricatures that distort and trivialize biblically based truth. And it galls some of us who wish that retailers would come to their senses. The stuff sells, so we have to put up with it and hold our tongues.

"Why does the devil get all the good music?" sang the Christian rocker a generation ago, and when Christians mimicked that old time rock-n-roll in order to attract youth, the result was more fluff, at least as I view most of it. And it has only gotten worse.

The impact of the junk is that it reduces Christianity to be viewed as just another craze or fad, simply another religion in the spiritual marketplace. The Scripture speaks of ultimate issues – life and death, heaven and hell – and it is not to be cast as another form of entertainment.

The self-help movement has also moved into the growing Christian fluff market, peddling sugar-coated biblical principles as a means to improve one's life. That it surely does is not in dispute, but self-improvement misses the point of Gospel proclamation.

If I had experienced the fluff and the rock-n-roll siren song generated by the Christian community in the early 1960s when my conversion was in process, it would have been one more barrier.

The last great obstacle – sin

It is all about sin. Sinning begins with the breaking of a known law of God. Perhaps it is lying. At first it is easy to lie, but once the wall is down, it is easier the next time and the next and the next. What was once so unnatural becomes natural and easy. Peter said a man is a slave to whatever has mastered him (2 Peter 2:19). Sin becomes a habit at some point, usually sooner rather than later, and after that it becomes an obsession. Beyond that, sinning becomes addictive. We sin more and more until finally we have to. Even when dire consequences become apparent, we cannot stop ourselves. We will behave badly for the smallest amount of pleasure. Indeed, some people are so mired in sin, depending so heavily upon some sin or another, that they are seemingly hopeless to fight the addiction. The thought of giving it up is so frightening that they will do almost anything to hold on to it. People will ruin their lives in order to avoid repentance. But worse – they will subject themselves to eternal ruin.

Sin is more often embraced than repented of. Indeed, sinful behavior will more quickly be tolerated, if not applauded, than abhorred. Yes, sin will even be championed, defended, and promoted in an effort to take the sting out of the conscience. This process is sometimes called "liberation." Within a classical definition of the word "liberal" is the notion of breaking free from the law of God. And the question comes: Breaking free to do what? The answer is simple enough: Sin.

We all have sinned and fallen short of the glory of God. We know it, too, and that is why the word "sin" is hated above all others. Mention the word in the wrong company and a riot could ensue. Talk about sin, and hearts are hardened, teeth are set on edge, consciences are stirred, passions are enflamed, and minds are closed. Even if the word is not defined with biblical accuracy, it will still get a reaction.

Preachers have been beaten, even killed, for mentioning the word in a sermon. Holy Hubert, who was famous in the Jesus Movement and routinely preached on the steps of Sproul Hall at the University of California's Berkeley campus, had all his front teeth knocked out, one by one, for telling the hippies they were "dirty rotten sinners." I know, because I acted as his unofficial bodyguard on more than one occasion. How those mellow pacifists became enraged over the word sin!

Before my conversion, it irritated me to hear the preacher say that because I had not trusted in Christ to save me, I was a sinner. He said I had to turn from my sin, and he made it sound as if everything I did was sinful.

I did not consider myself a sinner at all; "no worse than the average guy" was my motto. But as the months went by, although I do not know how, I became convinced I actually was a sinner. It is only with the advantage of hindsight that I can say that it was the work of the Holy Spirit. In any case, the truth became clear to me – I stood guilty before God.

At first I tried to clean up, do better, stop that and start this – the usual effort by a sinner who does not want to turn to Christ. I would put an end to one sin but discover two more or even start up a new one.

Sin and wickedness are related. In the dark recesses of our soul, sin is enshrined. But when the light of Jesus is cast on it, then the sin is seen for the utter corruption that it is. And this realization makes us most uncomfortable. I squirmed and wriggled, rationalized and compromised, but it was to no avail. Unable to find a way out on my own, my eyes were turned to Jesus, and I knew he was my only hope. Once I saw that Jesus was the Savior, I could not be kept from him. And this is usually how it is; Jesus becomes irresistible.

Sin is mysterious and powerful, blinding and addicting, a deadly spiritual cancer. Sin is so overwhelming that no one can overcome it. Only God can forgive, cleanse, and restore us. This great work took place on the cross where Jesus shed his blood and died in our place, taking the believer's sin upon himself and suffering the consequences. His resurrection is proof that our sin can be forgiven.

Before my conversion to Christ, my friends and I enjoyed the "fellowship of sin." We reinforced each other's sinful ways, approved of our mutual transgressions, sneered at the goodie-two-shoes and righteous Christians who weren't having any fun, and tried to convince ourselves that we were cool guys who really knew how to enjoy life. Once I came to Christ, I lost those friends who wanted to continue in this fellowship of sin. At the time I was hurt; I did not see that God was doing me a favor. The sinful fellowship was replaced by a better one, and it was God's plan, because I would never have been able to break free on my own.

The obstacle of sin is overcome by the inward working of the Holy Spirit. This holy and interior working of God helps us to repent, even gives us a hungering and thirsting after righteousness. Paul expressed it in these words: "For it is God who works in you, both to will and to work for his good pleasure" (Philippians 2:13). It will come to pass that we will gladly let sin go that we might have Jesus and his righteousness.

The real reason why I am a Christian

God himself removed the obstacles and overcame the problems. A young man, probably not unlike me, asked Jesus, "What good thing must I do to have eternal life?" (Matthew 19:16). Jesus essentially told the man that he could not do it on his own. Jesus' disciples overheard the conversation and were greatly astonished. They asked, "Who then can be saved?" (verse 25).

Jesus answered, "With man this is impossible, but with God all things are possible" (verse 26).

Left to myself, I only had obstacle piled on top of obstacle. I could not repent; I could not believe. But I wanted to, because I knew I must. In a moment, though, the obstacles were brushed aside. It was as though Jesus called me personally to himself. I wanted him. My lost condition threatened to destroy me forever, but I knew Jesus was the Savior. This truth, now clear to me, would not let me go.

Jesus seemed to stand before me calling out my name. The Savior who had borne my sin when hanging on a cross, the one who had shed his own blood to cleanse me of my sin, the one who had died and had been buried, the one who had risen from the dead and is alive for evermore – this Jesus called me to himself, and in a way I do not fully understand. And it was done right there and then.

This is why I am a Christian.

Two

Legalistic Grace

It sounds like a contradiction in terms – legalistic grace – but I have been coming across the sentiment, if not the term itself, in a number of different ways. However expressed, whether in print, sermon, television, radio, or conversation, it sounds very much like, "I am more of a Calvinist than you are."

At first I thought it was akin to an animal marking its territory, as we observe in dogs and cats. Perhaps the analogy is one of the old Calvinist guard not wanting to be marginalized or to not receive recognition for their heroic manning of the Reformed fort now that new recruits have volunteered for the front lines.

A Reforming Baptist

My own journey toward the Doctrines of Grace has been a slow one, little by little. This may have been due to the sheer glory of free grace, which must be absorbed over the course of time; or my slowness may have been due to the complexity of it all. I wonder, back in 1996, if I would have been rejected or even ridiculed for not embracing the complete collection of doctrine suddenly as a whole. But at that time and for some years to come, I knew no one who was a self-confessed Calvinist. Perhaps I was spared a rude awakening.

Coming from a Baptist background I had little exposure to the theology of those who had imbibed the traditional theologies handed down from Calvin, Luther, and others, mostly by way of John Knox. Instead, I learned from Billy Graham, Campus Crusade for Christ, C. S. Lewis, Watchman Nee, and other Arminian-leaning evangelicals. Then when I began reading Edwards, Owen, Spurgeon, Lloyd-Jones, I. Murray, J. I. Packer, R. C. Sproul, and others, my theological reeducation took a new and confusing turn.

In 1996 I was in the eleventh year of pastoring Miller Avenue Church in Mill Valley, California. I had begun research into the debate between Asahel Nettleton and Charles Finney, noted evangelists during American's Second Awakening, roughly 1799 to 1835. The research sparked a new understanding of the differences between Calvinistic and Arminian points of view. For twenty-nine years of professional ministry I had been a staunch Arminian, regularly teaching through Charles Finney's Revival Lectures, and John Wesley was one of my heroes.

Happily, there was no pressure from my congregation or denomination to toe any doctrinal line. The people I preached to and taught had little previous exposure to Reformed theology, so they took to it slowly. However, though it was some time before I even mentioned the name of John Calvin or Jonathan Edwards in a sermon or Bible study, some rejected even my feeble efforts to introduce clear biblical ideas like predestination and election. As pastor I had to be careful not to drive everyone off, remembering how haltingly I myself had progressed. The plain fact is that even after fourteen years of my consistent presentation of the Doctrines of

Grace,[1] only a fraction of the congregation are what I would call Reformed. Yet I am content with the progress.

Doctrinal Lists Added to the Basics

What I have been lately observing and experiencing with the emergence of the New Calvinists[2] is a pressure to accept a whole array of doctrines and positions beyond TULIP.[3] Many insist that to be a true Calvinist means adhering to much more that the famous five points. More or fewer of these additional doctrines are found on varying inventories: views on the inerrancy of the Bible; replacement theology – where the church replaces Israel; infant baptism and the Lord's Supper in the context of Covenant Theology; views of last things; women and their place in the church; cessationism – whether spiritual/charismatic gifts are in operation today; applications of church discipline; using the correct forms of worship, especially having to do with music; the place of historic confessions of faith; and the list could continue. The requisites can even include political or social positions. My discovery has been that not all of those who identify with the doctrines of Grace hold essentials in harmony. So often, adherents of the Reformed tradition make a particular list of required doctrines an all-or-nothing litmus test. Surely this attitude, while it may appear to be a committed one, is likely not the firmest foundation for growing in grace; such a doctrinaire attitude, at least in my experience, has seemed more like sectarianism than faithful biblical orthodoxy.

---

1   Doctrines of Grace, Reformed Theology, and Calvinism are roughly synonyms.

2   The term "New Calvinists" refers to those Christians who have more recently, say the last twenty years, and from denominations not rooted in the Reformation itself, begun to embrace the Doctrines of Grace.

3   The acronym TULIP refers to the five points of Calvinism: **T**otal Depravity, **U**nconditional Election, **L**imited Atonement, **I**rresistible Grace, and the **P**erseverance of the Saints.

Marking out territory? Or perhaps what I have been observing is a lack of grace along with a misunderstanding of the working of the Holy Spirit. We grow up slowly. We generally agree that wise parents do not demand that their young children demonstrate adult stature or maturity.

When asked to describe my theological position, I will say I am reforming rather than reformed. I have a long way to go in grasping all the ramifications of the Doctrines of Grace, since they deal with the greatness and glory of our Creator God. Early on, had I been instantly bombarded by the extent of the mercy granted me in Christ, I would have been overwhelmed, perhaps immobilized by the immensity of the realization. Yet, I run into people who have seemingly overnight become full five-pointers and are furthermore convinced of a number of extra points such as those listed above.

A Plea for Grace

This essay is a plea for those of us who have had the time and freedom to grow up into the Doctrines of Grace to extend this same privilege to others who are setting out on their journey.

We begin with grace, and we must continue the same way. Paul made this clear in his letter to the Galatian churches. Most Christians get the point easily enough when it comes to the salvation issue – works versus grace – and are convinced that they were helpless to attain it through their own efforts. But Calvinists, new and old, can be a blessing to those who are on the Reforming journey by not imposing unnecessary road blocks and by not demanding doctrinal conformity in a host of other issues. If we trust that God saves us in a sovereign way, may we not also expect that He will continue that process until the day of Jesus Christ?

Three

The Big Gamble

Most mornings I have to wait in line at the 7-11 store to buy my newspaper while people place their bets with the California lottery. A woman, anticipating my impatience as she took an inordinate amount of time making her choice, turned to me and defended her purchase of twenty lottery tickets. "I have to have something to look forward to."

I knew what she meant. All day long she could daydream about the millions she might win and the very notion of it would carry her through the day.

The woman at the store was not putting all of her money on the proverbial line, but many are putting far more than money on the line.

The Big Gamble

There is indeed an even bigger gamble than the lottery. Many are gambling that the grave is the end, the absolute end of life. My guess is that this is the most common, albeit unnamed, gamble of them all. The cessation of all life at the termination of the biological functions of the organism – this is the great hope of the godless. Nearly everyone who is committed to atheistic evolutionary schemes is hoping for this and counting on it. These people also reject any form of reincarnation taught by Hinduism or Buddhism. (I have observed, however, that they do not oppose Eastern religious ideas with as much energy as they do traditional Christian doctrines about the after-life.)

The "life ends at death" theory is powerful because of the abundance of evidence that seems to support it. And I admit there is plenty of information about the theory of random occurrences flowing from the physical sciences that seems to negate the necessity of a creator God. Evolutionary theories and hypotheses are being confirmed, apparently, regularly. These new discoveries seem to promise that any objections to evolutionary theories will be met and disabled at some point or another. There is no question that the doctrine of life as a random event that ends at death is attractive and powerful.

Where is the Proof?

No one committed to a life ends at death doctrine can be absolutely sure of the truth of it. It is an article of faith and nothing more. It is a gamble with monstrously high stakes – nothing less than eternity.

Suppose the theories that account for life postulated by agnostics and atheists are absolutely correct. Who is to say there is not a God who started it all? Even if the universe and the earth are as old as the theories suggest, does this do away with God? Certainly not! And again, if creatures resembling modern humans date back a million years, does this mean God did not specially create Adam and Eve? Certainly not! Science, many contend, can only discover the handiwork of God. Science is not intended to be a means of judging whether or not there is a God. Besides, experience teaches that scientific "truth" has a habit of changing. God, on the other hand, does not change. It is unwise to wager eternal life on presumptions founded on scientific theories.

Would a Miracle do?

Jesus told the story of a rich man who died and went to hell. Lazarus, a beggar who had lain at the rich man's door, also died, but he went to heaven. The rich man wanted God (Abraham in the story) to send Lazarus to his family to warn them about the terrible place of punishment and anguish. But Lazarus was not allowed to warn the rich man's family. God reminded him that they had the Scriptures, and that even if someone returned from the dead, they would not believe (Luke 16:19-31).

It is easy to sympathize with the rich man who thought a miracle would be persuasive. How many people have sworn: "If I could just have a sign, if I could just know for sure, then I would believe."

If God would only grant miracles, it would make it easier for all people to believe – or so it would seem. But God's way is faith that is placed in Jesus of Nazareth, who died in our place on the cross and then rose from the dead. Trust, surrender, love – this is how it works. If God were to reveal himself through miracles all the time, then he would be just another fact. We do not have a personal relationship with facts.

The End of the Story

The woman at the store buying the lottery tickets was not making an all-or-nothing bet, but so many are wagering eternity that the grave will be their end. Like the rich man in the parable Jesus told, they will be shocked to find that they have lost their bet. But the truth will be discovered only after the debt has been collected. Hell is a truth learned too late.

Four

Bill's Pain

Several years ago, I drove to Yuba City, California, to visit some former high school friends for two days of "catching up." On the morning of the second day, Bill said he didn't feel well. We thought it might be indigestion, since we had eaten hot peppers at a Mexican restaurant the night before. Two hours later Bill's pain was growing steadily worse.

Bill has periodic bouts with skin cancer and has had surgery to control sleep apnea, so he handles pain well, but this pain was making him very uncomfortable. We made a decision to take him to the emergency room at Rideout Memorial Hospital in Yuba City.

We arrived at the hospital about 10:30 AM, by which time the pain had Bill pleading for relief, but none was provided by the hospital staff. Nurses and a doctor prodded and poked Bill, hoping to determine the cause of the pain. After three hours, a nurse finally showed up with a hypodermic needle and gave Bill a light dose of a pain-killing drug. It barely touched the pain.

I watched my friend in agony for two more hours. He pleaded for another shot. The doctor and the nurses seemed indifferent, busily going about their business in a crowded emergency room. At one point I confronted the head nurse and pleaded for Bill's pain relief myself. I did not prevail; Bill continued to writhe in pain.

After a number of tests were run, a surgeon came into the room and told Bill he would have to have his appendix removed. He leaned over the bed and said, "Sorry about the pain, but if there is no pain, we would be hard put to find the cause. Painkillers hide disease."

Bill came through the operation fine and is back at work, although somewhat later than first projected, because the appendix was gangrenous. Much more delay might have cost Bill his life. But I learned something about pain and gospel preaching.

When unconverted people hear the gospel, they will sometimes feel rather uncomfortable. The Holy Spirit's convicting of sin can be most unpleasant. Hearing that repentance to God and faith in the Lord Jesus Christ are required may be quite shocking to the system. Pain! – a deep, existential, soulful pain may be the result. I have often seen this and too often I have sought to bring comfort to the anguished sinner. I have offered counseling, suggested therapy, and made affirming and supportive declarations. I have supplied a painkiller, not fully realizing that sin was causing the pain and that radical, spiritual surgery was needed to cut out the deadly disease.

A woman who had been attending our church for over two years made an appointment to see me. She had realized she was not a Christian and was greatly disturbed about it. As she sat in my office, she cried, describing the stress she was under and saying she was at her wit's end. My response was to comfort her. I opened my Bible to Romans 10:9-10 and read to her about confessing Jesus as Lord. I asked her if she wanted to confess Jesus, and she quickly said she did. I asked, "Do you believe God raised him from the dead?" She said, "Yes." "Okay then, confess that Jesus is your Lord." She did as I recommended.

That was five years ago. Within one month of that meeting, she left the church and has never returned. I have maintained contact with her, sending sermon tapes and newsletters through the mail. I came to realize that she was never converted. I gave her false and dangerous comfort. I did not see it at the time; I thought I was helping.

The process of conversion to Jesus may be difficult. Certainly we know that human childbirth is painful to the mother, and the baby usually comes out crying. Would we expect anything less in new birth? Sometimes people enter the kingdom of God violently. They struggle with coming to the light that exposes their sin, then they are confronted with letting go of sin that may have been in place for decades.

As I preach the riches of God's grace and mercy in Christ, I have to allow the Holy Spirit to operate; and some conditions are worse than others. In any case, I must not be too quick to comfort, as I do not want to mask the pain that is an indication of the disease. Physical pain will return when the affects of the drug wear off, but the falsely comforted sinner may never again feel the pain. Then their condition will be worse than before.

Five

Is Sin a Disease?

Sin is different from physical or emotional disease. The concept of sin implies personal responsibility for one's actions. Sin has to do with right and wrong. Sin presumes a holy God who, as Creator, has the authority to establish his law and punish lawbreakers. In the Bible, this holy God has revealed both what sin is and the fact that it must be atoned for and forgiven. Sin is not a disease that can be treated by medical science. Medication and therapy will not "cure" sin. Therefore, redefining sin as a disease is a mistake.

The Issue

Medical and psychiatric professionals, social engineers, representatives of the pharmaceutical industry, and politicians have, however, been increasingly convinced that one type of disease or another is at the root of many, if not most, of our personal and social problems. Even Alcoholics' Anonymous, an organization I greatly respect, considers alcoholism a disease.

Diseases can be medically treated. Usually there are signs and symptoms, then a diagnosis is made, and finally treatment is offered. Treatment by medication is becoming so ubiquitous, that we are in danger of becoming like the society depicted by George Orwell in 1984, in which everyone was required to swallow his daily dose of soma.

We are becoming too comfortable with the notion that people with problems are diseased, and we are consequently amenable to the use of mind-altering drug therapies (often accompanied with psychotherapy).

At the same time, many recoil at the suggestion that they are sinners. This was definitely true of me. As a long-time preacher of the gospel, I can say without hesitation that it is also true of many people who consider themselves Christians.

A Personal Story

My brother Gary was an army combat engineer in Vietnam in 1966-67. Prior to the end of his tour there, he encountered some serious trouble and was sent to a hospital in Japan, diagnosed with a psychiatric illness. After his return home, he regularly took medication and visited a Veterans' Administration psychologist. His medication consisted of inter-muscular injections of some type of drug. Gary eventually resisted the medication, because he was unable to function at the part-time plumbing job he had found. Fearing he would be fired, he stopped taking the injections. Within several weeks, however, in extreme desperation he killed himself.

I value the scientific advances made in the medical field and in no way disparage modern medicine and psychiatry. I also concede that there are instances in which drug therapy must be applied. Many people are greatly helped at some point in their lives through the use of therapy and drugs, either singly or in combination. But to attempt to turn sin into disease is an error, a most dangerous error indeed.

Sin: an Abusive Term?

To many non-Christians, sin is a discomforting, even irritating word, and I imagine most people would prefer it would disappear from common usage. Is it possible that the use of the word in public may one day be considered abusive? My experience demonstrates that this might be the case. Of course, there are those people, like some of the more extroverted television evangelists, who will use the word in a strident, unloving manner. However it is used, in whatever context, hackles rise at its mere mention. It is a stretch of the imagination at this point in history to predict that a lawsuit might result from the use of the word, but it may well come to that, if current trends continue.

The "S" Word

At the same time that some people are growing resistant to the "S" word, they are becoming comfortable with a disease paradigm. There is no shame or guilt in admitting, "I have a disease that makes me act this way. I need treatment; I need help." And this may be an accurate evaluation. But if a problem is actually moral in nature, to make a misdiagnosis is dangerous. To face up to guilt and shame may actually be the healthiest course to take. But avoiding personal, moral responsibility often feels like the path of least resistance and is therefore an attractive coping mechanism. It even comes close to the old excuse, "The devil made me do it."

Sin – a Spiritual Disease?

Sin is a disease, but it is spiritual in nature. It is like a cancer that works, usually unseen, inside a person. The symptoms of the sinful condition are the breaking of the laws of God, a rebellion against God and his Word, the Bible. Sin, when it has wreaked its havoc, yields death, and not merely physical death. Sin separates a person from God and heaven forever and must result in the unforgiven person being placed into hell. Obviously, sin is worse than any type of physical disease. For example, even if a Christian dies of a physical disease, he will still spend eternity with his Lord in heaven. On the other hand, a person who is healthy in every way and yet rejects Jesus and his gospel will die and be excluded from God's presence.

Do dysfunctional people commit more sin than "normal" people? I don't believe so, except to state that dysfunctional people's problems may be more apparent and may get them into more trouble with society. The Bible does not teach that only "troubled" people are sinners and fall short of the glory of God. No, we are all under the power and penalty of sin, whether we are mentally healthy or not.

Alienation from God yields a life of meaninglessness, loneliness, and despair. A person in rebellion against God will often experience depression, anxiety, and other mental/emotional symptoms as well as psychogenic physical illnesses. Although those symptoms may appear to be amenable to medical and psychiatric therapies, they are not.

Recall the medical model of disease-therapy: examination of signs and symptoms, diagnosis, and treatment. A person suffering from alienation from God may present various signs and symptoms of mental and psychogenic problems. But if the true, underlying cause of those symptoms is not recognized, then the correct diagnosis will be missed, and no type of medical or psychiatric treatment will prove effective.

A Terrible Misdiagnosis

If we are fooled into thinking that our problems, personal and social, can be exclusively treated by medical and psychiatric professionals, then we will be guilty of an awful misdiagnosis, and the real disease will continue undetected. Certainly, disease is a major human problem, and people are helped through the prescription of drugs and the use of therapy. And yes, we are fortunate to have these tools available. But it is as the old proverb says, "We cannot see the forest for the trees." The forest is sin, and even a good psychiatrist and Prozac, or whatever the best medicine has to offer, will not bring a cure for the disease of sin.

The Accurate Diagnosis and Remedy

Disease, despite its awful role in human history, is neither the fundamental nor the ultimate problem. Sin is. That is the diagnosis. And God himself has a remedy for sin. The Bible teaches that God the Father has sent his Son Jesus to be the means for the forgiveness of sins. On the cross, Jesus took the full punishment for the believer's sin upon himself. Jesus' suffering, death, and resurrection is the only remedy provided by God for sin and its consequences. Jesus himself is therefore the only treatment for spiritual disease and alienation. The Christian solution for sin is both humble and elegant: a simple trusting in Jesus for forgiveness.

The first step towards spiritual health is acknowledging sin. The first spiritual truth I learned was that I had sinned against God and stood guilty before him. Admitting my sin was not pleasant, and I resisted doing so for a considerable period of time. During that period I had a growing understanding that Jesus had died for my sin. The darkness of the reality of my sin was being countered by the light of God's grace and mercy. The sharp sense of my sin was the pain that led me to the healing of Jesus' atoning work on the cross.

Our God, the Great Physician, delights in forgiveness of sin and takes no pleasure in punishing the sinner. When we experience that forgiveness, we know God for the loving and good God he is. Sin, even the word itself, loses its power over us, because we know its terrible scourge has been removed forever.

Six

Lyman Beecher: How He Died

In *Preaching and Preachers*, Dr. David Martyn Lloyd-Jones referred to Lyman Beecher's (1775-1863) correspondence with and about Asahel Nettleton, the great preacher of the first half of the second Great Awakening in America. Beecher himself was greatly used of God in the early part of that awakening in his local church, and throughout his long ministry stood firmly for a Reformed faith over many controversies and trials. Lloyd-Jones recommended Beecher's biography for an understanding of the controversy between Nettleton and C. G. Finney that focused on the "new measures" employed by the new evangelist, Reverend Finney. The book was published by Harper & Brothers Publishers in 1865, and the two volumes of more than 1,000 pages reveal much about the life and ministry of Lyman Beecher. In reading it, I found much more than I was looking for, particularly in the material that covered the period before Beecher died. Four incidents especially stand out.

First, in retirement he attended Plymouth Church of Boston. During one of his last times ever to speak to a group, he "said feebly, 'If God should tell me that I might choose' (and then hesitating, as if it might seem like unsubmissiveness to the divine will) – 'that is, if God said that it was his will that I should choose whether to die and go to heaven, or to begin my life over again and work once more' (straightening himself up, and his eye kindling, with his finger lifted up), 'I would enlist again in a minute!'" (vol. 2, p. 552).

Being a preacher of the gospel, I thrilled to read those words. Beecher, aware of his diminished capacity, longed to depart and be with his Lord. Yet his love for his God-commissioned work was such that he would gladly do it all again. The great preacher, neither cynical nor discouraged by the unfaithfulness and error around him, still approached the pulpit to plead with sinners. Though an oft-wounded warrior, he was ready to take the field anew. Beecher's "feeble" words will long stay with me.

Second, when asked by a friend who was trying to rouse him from drifting to sleep, "Dr. Beecher, tell us what is the greatest of all things," he replied, "The answer, I quickly admit, I have memorized, since I know I will repeat it often: It is not theology, it is not controversy, but it is to save souls" (p. 555). Not that theology was unimportant; in fact, Beecher was a staunch defender of the faith once delivered to the saints. Furthermore, Beecher did not shy away from the controversies of his day. But the one great thing, the one that thrills me also, is to preach the gospel so that sinners might be converted.

Third, Beecher wanted to be buried next to his dear friend and long-time pastoral colleague, Dr. Taylor of Connecticut. The biography includes several references to Pastor Taylor, and contains dozens of their letters to each other. Though Dr. Beecher's memory was nearly gone, he remembered his old friend, and one day declared that he wanted to be buried next to him. He reasoned, "The young men [the students] will come and see where Brother Taylor and I are buried, and it will do them good" (p.555).

Beecher's burying place would be, he supposed, a last sermon of inspiration and encouragement to his students, probably referring to the students of Lane Seminary, into which Beecher had poured so much of his life and ministry. Even in that last detail of a resting place, Beecher had his eye on the glory of God. Could I be so concerned for the kingdom of God?

Fourth, knowing his earthly life was quickly coming to a close, he examined his own heart to see whether he was truly converted. His son and chief biographer, Charles Beecher, wrote, "Such was his sense of his imperfectness before the divine law, and such his profound humility before God, and such his sense of the solemnity of that great change that settles all forever, that he seldom or never spoke of his own condition with assurance, but only of prevailing hope on the whole" (p. 557).

Nonetheless, his daughter, Harriet Beecher Stowe, reported that he twice quoted these words of Paul toward the end: "I have fought a good fight, I have finished my course, I have kept the faith; henceforth there is laid up for me a crown, which God, the righteous Judge, will give me in that day;" and added, "That is my testimony; write it down; that is my testimony" (p. 557).

The examination completed, Lyman Beecher found his hope to be sure. I likewise hope, if possible, to make a similar examination now and then. For I, like Dr. Beecher, know that there is one great and important thing, and that is to know the Savior who is the resurrection and the life.

Seven

Taking Away Hope

The pro-gay position among some segments of the Christian community effectively deprives the homosexual of hope. These persons may be thinking they are reaching out in love to the gay community, but to theorize that a gay person is born that way and therefore cannot help being homosexual takes away hope. What may pass for a tolerant and accepting attitude among certain people, in fact condemns a person to what many gay people will admit is an unhappy, even desperate life. It also abandons people who are committed to homosexual behavior to a dreadful eternity.

A Frightening Passage

The passage I am about to quote from Paul's first letter to the first century church in Corinth is one that is feared, even hated, by those who assert they are both homosexual and Christian. It is a passage that has been vigorously attacked by pro-gay Bible commentators because of its uncompromising and powerful message. The meaning of the passage is simple and clear, yet it offers, in my view, a great deal of hope for the homosexual. The first part of the passage states:

Do you not know that the wicked will not inherit the kingdom of God? Do not be deceived: Neither the sexually immoral nor idolaters nor adulterers nor male prostitutes nor homosexual offenders nor thieves nor the greedy nor drunkards nor slanderers nor swindlers will inherit the kingdom of God (1 Corinthians 6:9-10).

I do not intend to browbeat nor scare anyone with the Bible. I want to present the hope we have in Christ.

An Examination of the Passage

"Homosexual offenders" is a translation of the Greek word *arsenokoite*, a word that Paul made up. (Paul made up or coined about 170 words that we find in his New Testament letters.) The word he used is a combination of arsenos, meaning male, and koite, meaning bed or couch. Paul found these words in Leviticus 18:22 and Leviticus 20:13, in the Greek translation of the Old Testament called the Septuagint. The Levitical verses forbid and condemn homosexuality. Paul put the two words together, because he wanted to describe men who had sex together. It is not homosexual prostitution or violent homosexual rape that the Law of Moses is concerned with, as is so often presented by pro-gay writers. No, the language is clear and straightforward – homosexual offenders or those who practice homosexuality, will not inherit the kingdom of God.

Homosexual behavior is not the only sinful behavior mentioned in the Corinthian passage. There is quite a long list, and I find some of my own sins there, too. There are the heterosexuals who are immoral and adulterers who have sex outside of marriage. There are those who worship gods who are not gods at all. There are thieves, greedy people, drunkards, slanderers, and swindlers listed – I find myself here. I have broken God's holy ordinance and therefore, barring a miracle, I will not inherit the kingdom of God. If God's Word is true, I am in desperate trouble.

Am I without Hope?

Since I find my sin(s) plainly listed in the passage, am I then without hope? In one sense, I have no hope, for I cannot do anything about changing what has already happened, and to make matters worse, I cannot be assured that I will not sin again sometime in the future. Though I do not want to sin and dishonor my Lord, it is more than likely that I will, because sin dwells within me (see 1 John 1:8-2:1-2). Yet I am not without hope; in fact, I am most hopeful. I know for a fact that Jesus has died in my place on the cross; I know he has taken all my sin upon himself, and that I can be forgiven, trusting in him as the Holy Spirit enables me. Certainly I can do nothing, but Jesus, raised from the dead, has already done what I cannot do. Indeed, he gives me his righteousness, even though I do not deserve it at all. This is the good news, the gospel.

The Proof of Hope

Earlier I quoted 1 Corinthians 6:9-10. But I stopped short of the real point Paul was making to the believers in Corinth. We need now to look at verse 11, because it contains proof of our hope:

> And that is what some of you were. But you were washed, you were sanctified, you were justified in the name of the Lord Jesus Christ and by the Sprit of our God.

In that Corinthian church were people like me – guilty of many sins, addicted to some, helplessly in the control of others. Yet, something happened to them, and Paul used three words to describe it – *washed*, *sanctified*, and *justified*.

Washed means being granted forgiveness. This involves a work of the Holy Spirit in applying the blood Jesus shed on the cross to the sinner. With the shedding of blood there is the forgiveness of sin, even sin like my own and also sin like homosexual behavior. I cannot forgive my own sin; neither can a church or a priest or a minister or anyone or anything else forgive sin. Only Jesus' blood can wash sin away. Did Jesus die on the cross and shed his blood to then withhold it from those who seek him? Not at all; remember that Jesus is the one who came to call not the righteous, but sinners to repentance. And the washing, the cleansing of the blood of Jesus actually brings us to a place of repentance. Washed, clean, forgiven – this is more wonderful than anything can ever be.

Sanctified, then, means to be set aside as belonging to Jesus himself. It is the result of the washing or cleansing power of God to remove all sin, and thus we are indwelt by the Holy Spirit. The sanctified are embraced by the Father and adopted into his own family. God's Holy Spirit actually lives within us, because that which prevented his doing so was overcome when our sins were forgiven. It is completely the work of God. He sets us aside, makes us holy, and begins to work within us both to will and to work for his good pleasure – which takes a whole lifetime.

Justified might well have been mentioned first or second, because it is the experience of conversion or the new birth. It happens as we are washed and sanctified. Where one begins and the other ends, we do not know. There is a mystery to it all, though it is very real at the same time. "Justified" might be defined as the sinner being restored to a condition of purity, as though no sin had ever been committed. It is by faith; it is grace; it is all a gift. Make no mistake, even faith is a gift; we really have none of it in ourselves. Rather, it is given to us. This is what we mean by grace: forgiveness and eternal life freely given, despite the fact that we are unworthy. This is illustrated for us in the words "new birth." We did not cause our own physical birth, and we cannot produce our spiritual birth. It is all a gift of God, not based on any kind or manner of work.

Giving back Hope

Those who accept the notion that they were born homosexual and that it is in their very nature to be homosexual may find hope in the words of Paul and in the experience of some of the Christians in the church at Corinth. There were homosexuals there, and they had turned away from homosexual behavior, though they might not have become heterosexuals. (Some today at any rate experience a change in their sexual orientation, but others do not, so it is not unreasonable to state that such might have been the case in Corinth).

A Special Appeal

To those who have loved ones who are gay, perhaps a son or daughter, I appeal to you that you do not take away their hope by agreeing that they cannot help but engage in homosexual activity.

There is a powerful tendency to overlook what the Scriptures teach and adopt a pro-gay stance, thinking we are standing with and supporting our gay loved ones. Many do this. It is, in the long run, better to love the person, be supportive in whatever means possible, but still refuse to validate the sinful behavior. This "tough love" may well prove to be both hopeful and redemptive.

Words of Hope

John said,

If we say we have no sin, we deceive ourselves, and the truth is not in us. If we confess our sins, He is faithful and just to forgive us our sin and cleanse us from all unrighteousness. I we say we have not sinned we make him a liar, and his word is not in us (1 John 1:8-10).

The pro-gay movement unwittingly takes away hope when it denies the sin of homosexual behavior. It takes away the possibility of being cleansed from unrighteousness, because no one confesses his sin who denies he is sinning. The promise of the Scriptures gives back hope. The following grand words of Paul provide for us a most fitting close to this essay.

May the God of hope fill you with all joy and peace as you trust in him, so that you may overflow with hope by the power of the Holy Spirit (Romans 15:13).

Eight

What is Happening to Hell?

I enjoy preaching on heaven; I dislike preaching on hell. Over the last twenty years, I have preached on hell once. Of course, I mention the doctrine every so often, but always in passing. This, I am convinced, is an error on my part, especially since the doctrine is rapidly falling into disrepute among those who once embraced it.

The Doctrine

As a doctrine, hell is solidly biblical. Certainly Jesus is abundantly clear on the reality of hell. In Matthew 25:41, Jesus states: "Then he will say to those on his left, 'Depart from me, you who are cursed, into the eternal fire prepared for the devil and his angels.'" Jesus concluded his remarks on the sheep and goats judgment by saying, "Then they will go away to eternal punishment, but the righteous to eternal life" (Matthew 25:46). Note that both heaven and hell are eternal. Those who believe in annihilation at death for non-Christians cannot have it both ways. If heaven is eternal, hell must be as well. (For further research on the subject, see Matthew 5:29; 8:11-12; Mark 9:43; Luke 16:19-31; 2 Thessalonians 1:9; Jude 6; Revelation 14:10-11; 20:10; 21:8.)

The biblical doctrine on hell has long been standard in mainstream Christianity. In his sermon, *The Great Assize*, John Wesley said, "It follows that either the punishment lasts forever, or the reward too will come to an end; no, never, unless God could come to an end, or his mercy and truth could fail." John Calvin wrote: "But the whole Scripture proclaims that there will be no end of the happiness of the elect, or the punishment of the reprobate."[1]

Cults and Sects

The Christian-based cults – the Jehovah's Witnesses, Mormons, Christian Scientists, and so on – deny the existence of an eternal hell and substitute some other circumstance that awaits the non-believer. This seemingly reasonable and charitable approach is one reason for the appeal of these cults. "Ah, the hated, unfair, and unreasonable doctrine of the professors of Christendom is shown to be false," the cults' ministers boast to the prospect. Is this a quote that has a citation reference?

The Adventists, a sect of Christianity (not now so doctrinally aberrant to earn the designation of cult) have long stressed the theory of annihilation. Their view is that life for the unconverted ends forever. (The Jehovah's Witnesses were influenced by this Adventist idea and changed it only slightly – Jehovah God slays all non-Witnesses and unfaithful Witnesses.) In any case, both the cults and certain so-called Christian sects, like the Adventists, deny the biblical teaching of an eternal punishment in hell.

The Church Growth Movement

Hell is not faring well with those churches that are committed to a contemporary marketing and branding strategy that downplays or ignores the embarrassing doctrine of hell.

---

1 *The Institutes*, Book III, chapter 25, section 5.

The doctrine simply will not help get people into the pews. Whether the ministers within the movement believe it or not is unknown and irrelevant. The determinant factor is that disquieting doctrines must be hidden from view, as they do not serve the greater purpose – getting people in the door. The result, though, is a slighting if not a downright rejection of the biblical truth. And this will ultimately serve neither the seeker nor the unchurched, because they will not realize their desperate need to come to Christ.

Summary

The operation methods of the cults and the contemporary efforts to attract the unchurched are already clear. However, there is something else afoot that is of greater concern.

Leave it to Ignorance

Philip Yancey, noted and respected among American evangelical Christians, admits in an article entitled, "The Encyclopedia of Theological Ignorance,"[2] that doctrines like an eternal hell bother him. He asks: "Will hell really involve an eternity of torment?" Essentially, he says that hell is a marginal doctrine, obscure and not plain. He wonders why the Bible does not give clear answers to the marginal doctrines.

Yancey differentiates between doctrines that are clear and those that are not. He appears theologically orthodox in general, but indicates that what the Bible says about hell is unclear. He includes the doctrine of hell in his "Encyclopedia of Theological Ignorance" as he does the subject of infant salvation. Yancey says that the issue of infant salvation is unclear in the Bible (perhaps so). Therefore, we should trust a loving and merciful God to do what is right and not attempt to clear up this marginal doctrine. He advises to take hell in

---

2 Christianity Today, 6 September 1999, Vol. 43, No. 10, p. 120.

the same way. The Bible is then, according to Yancey, unclear on the subject. This is amply demonstrated in the conclusion of his article.

I must insist that the other important answers about heaven and hell – who goes where, whether there are second chances, what form the judgments and rewards take, intermediate states after death – are inconclusive at best. Increasingly, I am grateful for that ignorance and grateful that the God who revealed himself in Jesus is the one who knows the answers.

Opaque?

By "opaque," Yancey means unclear. He does believe in heaven and hell, but in a way that negates or blunts their reality. A person persuaded by Yancey might well reason, "Hmm, I don't have to take the doctrine of hell seriously. I don't have to believe in it. I don't have to teach or preach it. I don't have to warn anyone of the danger of going there. I don't have to fear it myself – because it is not a clear Bible doctrine. Yes, I will leave it all up to God and, after all, he is merciful and loving."

What has Yancey done? He has muddled an important doctrine. He has told the watchman to come down from the tower, because there is no enemy. It is as if to say, "Why all this scary talk about judgment and hell? It is not clear, and whatever is not clear we should disregard and assign to The Encyclopedia of Theological Ignorance."

Accountability

Can we accept what Yancey advocates?

Personally, I cannot, though it would be nice if I could. If I could relax about the doctrine of hell and convince myself that it is a marginal doctrine, I would not need to warn and plead with the unconverted. It would reduce the risk of scaring them away. My reputation among the unconverted and especially the Christianized might improve. However, I cannot do it. I do not like the idea of hell any more than any other Christian. But the Scriptures teach it; the doctrine is beyond question. To say that the doctrine of hell is opaque is to both impugn the integrity of Jesus and deny the authority of Scripture. Worst of all, it gives the unconverted false hope and comfort. How very dangerous; how very awful.

Emotional and Personal Reasons to Reject the Doctrine of Hell

Hell is a doctrine that Christians find difficult, not usually for theological nor biblical reasons but for emotional and personal reasons. I understand this.

My mother, who gave me life and loved me unconditionally, died not trusting in Jesus. As best I could, I shared the gospel with her, but she steadfastly rejected it. Moreover, my wife's family, siblings, parents, and grandparents are strangers to the promise of eternal life in Christ. So, I have many reasons why I might want to obscure the doctrine of hell. How comforting it would be to downplay hell, perhaps develop a theology of second chances, and accept the notion that beloved family members could yet find safety and salvation in heaven apart from grace, or even suggest some sort of universalism. While one of these notions might ease some pain and anxiety, it would do no one any good.

A dear friend recently confessed to me that he was terribly upset that his father might die in his sins and be condemned to hell. I was actually tempted to comfort him by minimizing the reality of hell. Would it have helped? Would it have been the honest thing to do? As Christians, we must face these hard truths. We did not make them up, and whether we believe them or not does not and cannot alter the truth.

A Clear and Present Duty

Preachers (and we are all preachers) of the whole counsel of God and the fullness of the gospel have to warn of hell. However unpleasant it is, however many people designate us to be hopeless literalists, the truth must be made clear. Ours is a higher duty than to falsely comfort the unconverted as Philip Yancey has done.

Preachers of the gospel have been made watchmen who will give account of their ministry.

> When I say to the wicked, "O wicked man, you will surely die," and you do not speak out to dissuade him from his ways, that wicked man will die for his sin, and I will hold you accountable for his blood. But if you do warn the wicked man to turn from his ways and he does not do so, he will die for his sin, but you will be saved yourself" (Ezekiel 33:8-9).

To and From

If I did not believe that the unconverted would end up in hell, I doubt I would preach much of a gospel. What would be the point? What would I, the watchman, need to warn about? If there is nothing to be saved *from*, why preach a gospel of salvation? Someone might respond, "Well it is still better to have faith and be positive, even if it is for this life only." Is that really all we have to offer? How can I follow the example of Jesus and do anything he commanded me in this life, if he has lied to me about heaven and hell? I would have to assume other falsehoods as well. No, we are saved *to* and *from* something. We are saved *to* being in Christ now and enjoy the abundant life he gives us, and then finally *to* being with him in heaven. And we are saved *from* being separated from him forever in hell. This is an essential part of the gospel.

What Happens to Hell is not Marginal

What will the minister who does not believe in hell preach? Perhaps he will deliver sermons about justice, self-improvement, the poor and disadvantaged, and more – all important subjects. But since there is a judgment that follows the resurrection of the just and the unjust, it will be an incomplete ministry. As Jesus said, "What good will it be for a man if he gains the whole world, yet forfeits his soul?" (Matthew 16:26).

I am not suddenly going to become exclusively a "hell-fire and brimstone" preacher. But I will preach on it as occasion arises; I will warn of a terrible judgment upon all those outside of Christ that will surely result in an eternal hell. I will preach it, because it is the truth, and people need to know the truth so they would seek him out and be found by him.

Nine

It Amazes Me

It amazes me that anyone around here comes to Christ at all. And it is no surprise that less than 2% of my fellow citizens of Marin County, California, attend church services on Easter Sunday.

From the Newspaper

Here are the thumbnail sketches of items I read in the *San Francisco Chronicle* recently [originally meaning pre-2000]. Two teenage brothers in Redding, California shot two homosexuals to death, because it was their "Christian" duty to do so. An ex-Protestant minister was in town to promote his new book on Tibetan Buddhism. A Catholic priest in Santa Rosa was arrested for molesting altar boys over the course of fifteen years and made a plea bargain with the district attorney's office. A Baptist pastor in the South Bay, convicted of embezzling church funds, was sent to state prison. The daughter of a Protestant minister, after recovering lost childhood memories, sued her now retired father for sexual abuse. A professional football player, active in Christian ministry, received three years probation for drug use and sales. An archaeologist made fun of the Bible's account of Noah's

Ark in a lecture at a local college. A school board in a southern state passed a resolution prohibiting fundamentalists from displaying the Ten Commandments in schoolrooms. An Alabama judge's decision that evolution cannot be taught in the schools was overturned. The pastor of a Pentecostal church in Oakland disappeared with the money raised to get the congregation ready for Y2K. A local radio preacher announced that Jesus would not return on 1 January 2000, but on 1 January 2001. You don't even want to hear about the previous week!

It amazes me that anyone is ever converted around here. But, once in a while, someone is. I know this is California, but what is reported in the *Chronicle* often makes newspapers across the country. And what I reported about the newspaper items is nothing compared with the crazy things shown on "Christian" television and radio. (I won't discourage you by describing them.) Then there are the surrounding churches themselves. When I talk about it to others in different parts of the country, they think I am making it up or am at least exaggerating. Well, believe me or not, here is some of it.

Local Churches

First, let me tell you how I know. Some people around here, although very few, are church shoppers. That is, they shop around for a church to belong to. Or, they attend churches for short periods due to some special lecture series or concert that is given. Or, a disgruntled former member returns with tales to tell. These people pass through our own church and sometimes talk about their experiences elsewhere. I therefore get a good idea of what is happening. I also know most of the ministers around here and occasionally meet with them and compare notes.

Several pastors of local churches do not consider themselves Christians and say so from the pulpit. One is a Hindu, another is a self-described agnostic, and a third is a post-modern seeker after truth wherever it might be found. I am not telling tales here, nor am I passing on negative information. These pastors are proud of their spiritual attainments. Their churches are the largest and wealthiest in southern Marin County.

The Homeless

Then there are the homeless. One wears a red-hooded sweatshirt so that he will always be covered in the blood of Jesus. I have seen him recently in front of the 7-11 store with the hood pulled closed across his face. Many local people know he does this to keep the demons out (he has made this clear himself and does so as a "witness"). He imagines that he is a glamour expert and frequently approaches women with tips on how they can make themselves look beautiful for Jesus.

Another is continually running for various local political offices, and on the ballot he lists his occupation as "minister." On television interviews, panel discussions, and debates he makes a mockery of Christianity and the Bible with his strange and deranged comments. He is widely known for carrying around a huge copy of a Bible that was printed in the early 1500s.

I am not proud of telling of the peculiar nature of our area, I am not trying to raise money to combat the evil around me, and I do not consider myself to be a better minister than any other. It is simply that given it all, I am amazed that anyone ever becomes a Christian.

Blind and Bound

Another reason why I am amazed anyone ever trusts in Jesus is that Satan has blinded the eyes (the mind) of the unconverted, as described by Paul in 2 Corinthians 4:4.

Satan, the god of this age, blinds in ways we do not understand. Jesus said Satan uses pretended signs and wonders in order to deceive (Matthew 24:24).

Our sin also keeps us from Christ. Because of this, we hate the light of Jesus and will not come to him out of fear that our sins will be exposed (John 3:19-21). Paul says that sin produces spiritual death, so we cannot know anything of Jesus and his truth (Eph. 2:1; 1 Cor. 1:18; and 2:14).

It is Amazing Grace

That anyone is ever converted both amazes and somewhat discourages me. And I do not see things getting any better (barring an awakening). However, even without revivals and awakenings, some are being converted. I see it in my own church at Miller Avenue. In fact, God is constantly calling to himself those he has ordained to eternal life. I take great courage, hope, and confidence from Acts 13:48, which states, "All who were appointed for eternal life believed." Though Paul's fellow Jews often rejected the gospel, Gentiles plus some fellow Jews, did come to Jesus in this case and others.

Jesus "came to seek and to save what was lost" (Luke 19:10). He searches for us like the shepherd does for the lost sheep and the woman does for the lost coin. Those who are found are like those received as the father does his lost son.

It is not my practice to wring my hands and lament over the lack of success of the gospel. My task is to preach the gospel and know that God will save those whom he will. No one can come to Jesus unless he or she is drawn by the Father. But by the preaching of Jesus, the Father does just that. "Faith comes from hearing, and hearing through the word of Christ" (Romans 10:17).

What God did for me, he will do for others. Despite my deadness, blindness, fear, and error, he saved me. Yes, it amazes me!

Ten

The Real Reason

For nearly thirty years I assumed a person could decide to become a Christian. However, it became clear that salvation was on the basis of grace through faith – gifts of God. This is evident from many passages of Scripture, such as Ephesians 2:8-9: "For by grace you have been saved through faith. And this is not your own doing; it is the gift of God, not a result of works, so that no one may boast."

Faith and Grace

I knew grace was a gift of God, but I had assumed faith rose out of the individual. I did not see that faith was a gift as well. But grace comes through faith and both are gifts. Faith cannot be a work, or grace could not be grace. But this is more of a problem for many than I imagined! The biblical understanding of grace is ignored or twisted, while at the same time almost everyone knows the words to the great hymn "Amazing Grace."

The Real Reason

The real reason for this I am convinced has to do with fear: fear that something so vital is beyond our control. Salvation, forgiveness, and eternal life are all ultimate issues, and all come through grace; they are given and cannot be acquired or earned. So then, what if God does not give grace? What if God chooses to predestine to hell rather than heaven? It is a fearful prospect, or so it appears at first. But it is fear, perhaps demonically inspired fear, that is behind the hostility directed towards the good message of grace.

The Fear of God

Scriptural passages teach that the fear of God is the beginning of wisdom. The kind of fear of God encouraged in the Bible is a respect, honor, and reverence for the Almighty. Fear of grace, though, is entirely different. This fear reasons, "If I cannot choose God, and he does not choose me, I am lost." This is a great and terrible fear.

Good News!

It is good news that I cannot choose God. It is good news that God chooses me. Why? It is simply because I cannot believe; I have no capacity to do so. Not only am I dead in my trespasses and sins, but the best I can do, as far as faith is concerned, is to generate within myself some measure of positive thinking. Though positive thinking is often presented as the nature of faith, it is not at all. And most of us are failures at being positive all the time, or even some of the time. I may be able to be so for a while, but I soon give way to doubt and pessimism. I cannot stay focused in my thinking. So then, if my salvation depends upon my ability to be positive, I am doomed and will be gripped with a powerful fear.

Love Replaces Fear

Love and fear are opposites. Remember the song: "Jesus loves me, this I know, for the Bible tells me so."? Not only does God love me, but he also does not wish me to perish but to come to him for forgiveness. He is actually seeking sinners; he is knocking on the door, calling out our name. He has come to seek and save those who are lost. "In this is love, not that we have loved God but that he loved us and sent his Son to be the propitiation for our sins" (1 John 4:10); and "But God shows his love for us in that while we were still sinners, Christ died for us" (Romans 5:8). The truth is, God's love overcomes our fear.

Come to Jesus

Here is both the heart of the matter and the reason for strong hope and confidence: "All that the Father gives me will come to me, and whoever comes to me I will never cast out" (John 6:37). For the person who senses a fear of God and hostility towards grace welling up inside, this is not from God. Come to Jesus who is seeking you, loves you, and longs to be your Savior.

Eleven

Soul Confusion

The March 16, 1999 television chat show, *Larry King Live*, featured five panelists: Robert Thurman, professor of Buddhism studies at Columbia University; Marianne Williamson, New Age author and spokesperson for the spiritist-channeled Course in Miracles; Rabbi David Aaron, expert on and proponent of Kabbalah, an occult/mystical/gnostic interpretation of Judaism; Deepak Chopra, charismatic spokesperson for a popular version of Hindu monistic thought; and Franklin Graham, head of Samaritans Purse, a Christian humanitarian organization, and son of Billy Graham, the renowned American evangelist.

What is the soul?
Though these five differed on many points, they seemed to reach a consensus in understanding "soul." In fact, Deepak Chopra voiced agreement with Graham's understanding of the soul. We have long heard Billy Graham say words like: "You have a soul and it will go to heaven or hell when you die."

According to this idea, the soul is a mysterious, spiritual and immortal part of the human being that leaves the cold, dead body at death. Those on Larry King's program who believed in some form of reincarnation were able to agree together about the soul though, from their own traditions, they might have used other symbols to express the same thing.

Due to a revival of Geek philosophy in the fourth and fifth centuries A.D., Greek dualism infiltrated the Christian Church mainly through the work of Thomas Aquinas and his Summa Theologica, which became the fountainhead of Catholic theology throughout the Dark Ages. Greek dualistic thought posits the theory that the mind, spirit and soul are good, even divine, while on the other hand, the body, flesh and matter are bad, the repository of evil. So it was the soul that mattered, the soul that needed saving; the body was simply a temporary prison for the soul.

Soul and Self

Confusion concerning the nature of the soul has a powerful influence among the people of Mill Valley where I minister. Though the doctrine is not biblical, and is absent from the teaching of the early church, the idea that the soul is the focus of evangelistic efforts persists in many Christian traditions. Franklin Graham was concerned about the soul. He should have been concerned about the whole person; body, mind, soul, and spirit.

So many in my community believe in reincarnation that Graham's doctrine on the soul would not be troublesome for them. The soul? Well, they say, it needs purifying and experiences endless lifetimes anyway. These people do not like to think that they will be resurrected to stand before the judgment of God. "My soul" is one thing; "myself" is another.

Total Resurrection

The biblical doctrine is one of bodily resurrection, not the floating away of an immortal soul. We are whole, integrated beings, though the Bible writers spoke variously of mind, heart, body, flesh, spirit and soul for the sake of emphasis. A person is all of these and more, a whole being responsible to God in the totality and indivisibility of his nature. What we are in total will be raised from the dead, either to eternal life or eternal death. We do not have immortality in and of ourselves. This truth is found in 1 Corinthians 15:53: "For this corruptible must put on incorruption, and this mortal must put on immortality" (NKJV).

Soul confusion must be countered by the truth of the resurrection, even if it means parting from long-established ways of thinking and preaching. Let us not give the unconverted comfort by implying that they have only some ethereal soul to be concerned about.

Additional Commentary

Probably more Christians than not hold to the idea of a soul that is somehow inside the body and survives biological death. This is understandable, because the Church in the fourth century incorporated the idea into its theology, and it has remained ever since.

Flourishing in the fourth century was a revival of Greek philosophy, mainly dualism of the Neo-Platonic or Neo-Aristotelian varieties.[1] Over a millennium later the reformers such as Martin Luther and John Calvin, both ministers (priests) in the Roman Catholic Church, retained their Church's doctrine of the soul, despite expounding salvation

---

1   Dualism, among other things, viewed the body as bad, even evil, while the mind, spirit, soul, were good and connected to the divine. The body then became the prison house of the soul, which supposedly pre-existed and entered human bodies, transmigrated or left them upon death. The Eastern concepts of karma and reincarnation are dependent upon this understanding of soul.

by grace through faith alone. Only the more radical reformers, the Anabaptists, looked for their theological foundations further back in history before Augustine of Hippo (A.D. 354-430), the great Pauline theologian, who incorporated the construct of the separate existence of the soul in the human being. The famous Augustine, one of my heroes of the Church, nevertheless was steeped in Greek philosophy and blended the dualistic concept of the soul into his Christian views. Thomas Aquinas (A.D. 1225-1274), another great theologian, then included the Greek influenced doctrine of the soul in his Summa Theologica, minus the portion about the transmigration and pre-existence of the soul that was common to Greek philosophy.

The Christian Protestant denominations originating out of the Reformation inherited the concept of the soul. From Luther comes the Lutheran denominations; from John Calvin and John Knox come the Reformed and Presbyterian churches, followed by the Congregational churches, the Anglican Church, and by extension both American Episcopal and Methodist churches, plus all the offshoots from these denominations. Not all the Baptists, who followed the Anabaptists, rejected the Greek influenced soul view, but many did. Pentecostals and charismatics hold a variety of concepts about the soul.

Biblical passages having to do with the soul

We first encounter the word "soul" in Genesis 2:7: "Then the LORD God formed the man of dust from the ground and breathed into his nostrils the breath of life, and the man became a living creature." And the reader would be correct in protesting, where is the word "soul?" The version quoted is the English Standard Version (hereafter ESV) and has replaced "soul" with "creature." And why? Because "creature" is a better rendering of the Hebrew nephesh than soul.

The point is that God created a human being.

The King James Version (hereafter KJV) and older English versions of the Bible translate nephesh as "soul," and so the term has stuck. Furthermore, soul has come to acquire something close to the idea of "ghost," and not because of anything biblical. And in fact, in Job 11:20 and Jeremiah 15:9, the KJV translates the Hebrew nephesh with ghost.

In Deuteronomy 6:5 we find the greatest of the commandments: "You shall love the LORD your God with all your heart and with all your soul and with all your might." The Hebrew word for soul here is from nephesh. The point of the commandment, however, means that we are to love God with all of us, and thus the bringing together of three words that were commonly used to describe different aspects or characteristics of all that is human – heart, soul, might.[2]

Many Christians, including editors of biblical texts, unreasonably retain how the KJV translated many words, due to the extreme, yet appropriate popularity of that version of the Bible; therefore, the word "soul" pops up frequently in the Old Testament. But it means creature, person, or living being, and it does not refer to something ethereal and separate from a body. It is better said that a human being is a soul. To say a human being has a soul is not a biblical construct. And those who disagree I advise to investigate the issue and not to simply rely on tradition.

There are literally dozens of passages in the Old Testament where it is clear that the English word soul really means person. For the purposes of this book, two examples will be given that are characteristic of the lot. The first is from Exodus 1:5, and the KJV is, "And all the souls that came out of the

---

2 Jesus quotes Deuteronomy 6:5 and inserts the word "mind" along with heart, soul, and strength. See Mark 12:30 and Luke 10:27. Thus Jesus interprets the fulfilling of the greatest commandment to include the mind; thus love of God is conscious and thoughtful.

loins of Jacob were seventy souls: for Joseph was in Egypt already." Two times the word "souls" appears, and in both cases the Hebrew word is nephesh. Now the same verse in the ESV: "All the descendants of Jacob were seventy persons; Joseph was already in Egypt" (Exodus 1:5). In one instance, nephesh is translated "descendants" and in the second "persons." The ESV gives the most natural of the translations and is more accurately reflective of the Hebrew writer's mindset.

The second example is from Psalm 6:3-4, and the KJV is, "My soul is also sore vexed: but thou, O LORD, how long? Return, O LORD, deliver my soul: oh save me for thy mercies' sake." In both cases soul is nephesh. The same verse in the ESV reads, "My soul also is greatly troubled. But you, O LORD--how long? Turn, O LORD, deliver me for the sake of your steadfast love." Nephesh is the Hebrew word translated "soul" in "my soul" and "me" in "deliver me." In the first instance the ESV translators have the emotional experience of the writer in mind – King David's emotional state of mind to be exact – and so the term "soul" meets the literary requirement to better convey emotion. In the second instance "me" is more appropriate, as David is directly referring to his person. This second instance from the Psalms illustrates a wide range of translation possibilities, but "soul" speaks to us in a poetic manner.

The Greek translation of the Hebrew Scripture known as the Septuagint or LXX is a translation made by Jewish scholars in Alexandria Egypt in the early part of the second century before Christ. In it, psyche is used in place of nephesh in both passages, Exodus 1:5 and Psalm 6:3-4, and is consistently the case throughout the translation.

Turning our attention now to the English versions of the New Testament, we see that psyche is sometimes translated "soul." With the exception of the Gospel of Luke and the Book of Acts, the New Testament was written by Jews who inherited the Jewish understanding of the soul. Jews did not believe, in complete distinction from the Greeks, that the soul was anything other than the whole person. Old and even new translations of the New Testament tend to pull toward the KJV and translate psyche as soul. Again, we are looking at tradition.

Let us consider a couple of examples. One is Matthew 2:20: "Saying, Arise, and take the young child and his mother, and go into the land of Israel: for they are dead which sought the young child's life" (KJV). "Life" is psyche, so the KJV used the proper word, thus revealing that the KJV translators knew the correct translation. The ESV also has "life" here. We will remember that psyche is the Greek equivalent for the Hebrew nephesh.

A second example is Matthew 10:39: "He that findeth his life shall lose it; and he that loseth his life for my sake shall find it" (KJV). "Life" in both places is psyche.

Mark 3:4 is helpful: "And he saith unto them, Is it lawful to do good on the sabbath days, or to do evil? to save life, or to kill?" Here "save life" uses psyche for life and is the antonym for "kill." Obviously, Jesus has in mind a person and not a ghost, soul, or something else of an ethereal nature, which, according to some, could not be killed anyway.

And this is the problem with importing into the Judaeo/Christian Scripture the concept of a soul that does not die or cannot be extinguished. The biblical worldview is resurrection. Jesus was resurrected; even He had no soul that survived the crucifixion. Furthermore, when Jesus cried out, "Father, into your hands I commit my spirit!" (Luke 23:46), "spirit" in the sentence is from the Greek pneuma and can be translated spirit, breath, or wind. It was essentially an idiom, a statement that would have been well understood by those who heard Him and that meant simply, "Father, as I am now dying I trust in You" – a final confession of faith.

Let us close with 1 Corinthians 15:45. First the KJV: "The first man Adam was made a living soul; the last Adam was made a quickening spirit." Soul is psyche and spirit pneuma. The ESV translates it, "The first man Adam became a living being; the last Adam became a life-giving spirit." Adam was a person, not something without a body. Jesus is the last Adam, the one who brought life and not death.

Twelve

"You're a Fundamentalist, aren't you?"

I did not want to answer this question. No good would come of it anyway. The question, an accusation really, had been slung at me like a stone intended to wound, and it came from a person who would not likely hurl a racial or ethnic epithet at anyone.

People have accused me of being a fundamentalist. I use the word accuse, which may not be a completely accurate description of the motive of every speaker, but some words sound like a negative insult in certain contexts, whether the speaker intends it as such or not. When used as a label or stereotype, it may reveal a deep-seated prejudice, even anger.

Few today know what the word means, and most do not know the history of fundamentalism; it is therefore a word used in ignorance to diminish, demean, and defame any Christian who takes a stand for the Bible and Christ, regardless of whether he or she is a true fundamentalist. Many Christians today would not appreciate the fundamentalist label being applied to them. The truth is, I do not like it myself. However, if I look at how the original definition of fundamentalism should be understood, then I have to admit that, indeed I am one.

The Original Definition and History

At the beginning of the twentieth century, when anti-Christian liberalism was on the rise, especially in the universities, some American conservative Christians formulated the fundamentals of the faith in an attempt to counter the growing liberalism in the seminaries, denominational headquarters, and churches. They declared a faith in the inspiration and authority of the Scriptures, and affirmed the deity, blood atonement, bodily resurrection, and return of Jesus. Except that evangelicalism was grouped together with fundamentalism in the view of academics, there is nothing too controversial here. The points stated above are actually normal biblical views; that is, if one takes the Bible seriously at all. So why the fuss about being a fundamentalist?

One problem was that the early fundamentalists began fighting among themselves as to who was the purest in doctrine and practice. It became quite vicious, and the squabbles spilled over into the media. Then, one group separated from another, followed by more splits, and the fabric of denominationalism was literally coming apart at the seams.

Strong Accusations

The liberal contingent of American Christianity even accused the fundamentalists of aiding and abetting the Axis powers during World War I because of premillennial, dispensational end-times views. These views predicted a world getting worse and worse, and when this appeared to be happening, the fundamentalist scolded, "See, I told you so." It was certainly untrue that the fundamentalists supported America's enemies, but bad publicity has an impact regardless.

The famous 1925 Scopes Trial, otherwise known as the "Monkey" trial, that pitted William Jennings Bryan, a Christian, against the renowned criminal lawyer, Clarence Darrow, was widely reported in the American press. The issue was whether evolution should be taught in the public schools. Bryan, an educated and gentlemanly defender of the Christian faith, and constantly defined as a fundamentalist, came off less than second best to Darrow, with the result that fundamentalism, along with all of Bible-believing Christianity, was made a laughing stock around the world. In fact, fundamentalists were often called Bryanites. Many Christians, I suspect, were scandalized by it all, and many more turned away from Christianity altogether. This legacy continues into the modern age.

False Predictions

But there is still more. Some fundamentalist preachers, convinced they had the correct understanding of end-time prophecies, were sure that Mussolini (then later, Hitler, and still later, Stalin) was either the beast or the Antichrist of the Book of Revelation. After the process of history demonstrated the fallacy of such predictions, the fundamentalists lost a lot of credibility. Predictions are still being made that eventually fail and thus continue to cause difficulties.

Politics!

The fundamentalists developed social and political agendas as well. Soon, becoming a Christian also meant adopting a particular political affiliation or outlook – almost always of a conservative persuasion. Bible-believing Christians, it was thought, voted in a particular way. Fundamentalism took on science, too, hoping to counter the growing influence of evolution. This sometimes resulted in a pseudo-science, which was often laughable. According to hard-core fundamentalists, true Christians had to consider science as an enemy of the faith.

Some fundamentalists thundered against things like hair

and clothing styles and various forms of popular entertainment, with dancing often singled out as being particularly evil. They sharply rejected the use of alcohol and tobacco, and some historians blamed them for the American Prohibition. The list goes on.

The fundamentalists were portrayed as meddling with people's private lives, and it did not go down well in either the media or over the back fence. Fundamentalist came to be a word applied to people who were considered narrow, bigoted, backward, uneducated, and boring.

Accusation by Analogy

Even in today's parlance, religious terrorists of any stripe, color, or creed are called fundamentalists: Hindus, Muslims, even Buddhists who attack and kill other people for any reason are labeled extremists or fundamentalists. Every crazy cult that makes the news can receive the fundamentalist tag.

Does anyone want to be called a fundamentalist? Most would say, "No!" And even the threat of being called one is enough to scare people away from churches, a desire to read the Bible or entertain a spiritual thought that might be vaguely Christian in character. People will even be embarrassed to say anything that might vaguely connect them with things Christian and biblical, while at the same time, the same stigma is not attached to Eastern, alternative, and pagan religious practices and ideas. This is an unhappy and unnecessary state of affairs.

Survival of the Accused

Since I am often asked if I am a fundamentalist, and since I have to deal so often with the emotional stress of facing the fundamentalist branding in face-to-face confrontations, perhaps I could pass on some of my survival techniques.

The bottom line is: I don't much care what I am called

personally. I would like to think my inner strength is developed well enough to take the name-calling. Jesus' strength is sufficient for me. He was accused of all sorts of things, so why should I think I would escape unthinking, unkind, even cruel accusations? People will call me strange things and think of me in ways that do not reflect who I really am – this goes with the territory on which I stand.

I stand for the fundamentals of the faith. However, I am not necessarily going to stand behind all that has been identified as fundamentalism. For instance, I do not expect, much less demand, that society as a whole adopt social and political agendas that I embrace. I have accepted that I live in a pluralistic society, which is essentially post-Christian. By this, I mean that Christianity is rapidly becoming a minority faith, and our society is not governed by a biblical ethic. I must recognize this or I will be forever disappointed, discouraged, and angry. In addition, I am satisfied with people forming their own conclusions about how they will live their lives. Even when I see actions that I think are less than biblical, I will not react with judgment against people who are not interested in adhering to the biblical standard. But I hope, and know to some degree, that believers will grow up to the fullness of Jesus as God works his will and ways into their lives. Living in the midst of this fallen world, I know I am in it but not of it. I am careful to keep my "light" out in the open and burning as brightly as possible, so I am not going to slink away with my tail between my legs.

Furthermore, I am careful to fight the right battles. I will even let go of some so-called important issues, because they are not central to the core gospel of Christ.

In the right circumstances I present a history of fundamentalism to people of good will who have a genuine interest in the subject. I do not "cast pearls before swine," yet I have found many people appreciate a new understanding of the history of fundamentalism as well as evangelical and reformed Christianity. Mainly, I am concerned that people do not close themselves off from Jesus for fear of being branded a fundamentalist. How sad that an unfounded fear, augmented with historical ignorance, should result in a person being cut off from God's love and salvation.

The Better Label

What labels do fit me? I prefer simply "Christian." But I will accept evangelical, Protestant in the Reformed tradition, conservative, and even fundamentalist if I can set the historical context. I am a Christian, because God the Father opened my eyes, my ears, and my heart to hear Jesus' voice calling out to me. He saved me. He washed all my sin away. He gave me the gift of eternal life. His Spirit indwells me. I belong to him. He made me a part of his family, the Church, both in heaven and on earth. This is who I am. Hang whatever other label you want to on me. I know who I am.

Thirteen

What Can the Unconverted Do?

After twenty-nine years of ministry with an Arminian viewpoint, I underwent a theological transformation. Much of the change was the result of studying the first and second Great Awakenings in America. I am now "reforming," and it has been quite a jolt to the church I pastor. Some have left the church, some have been converted, and yet others have come to the conclusion that they are unconverted, but they remain in the church fellowship. What these precious seekers can do to become converted is a critical issue for me right now.

What can they do?

I used to have an easy answer to this question. "Pray this sinner's prayer," was my usual response. Now I know that the result will probably be a false conversion, or, as I like to say, "Christianization," rather than genuine conversion. But can I have any response at all and still be true to the Reformed tradition, which I believe more closely adheres to the biblical model? I believe so.

The unconverted may seek God, his kingdom, and his righteousness.

The Problems

Two problems must be addressed. First, the unconverted are dead in their trespasses and sins (Ephesians 2:1) and thus have no will to do anything but continue in rebellion against God. Second, "The god of this world has blinded the minds of the unbelievers, to keep them from seeing the light of the gospel of the glory of Christ, who is the image of God" (2 Corinthians 4:4). Between sin and Satan, the unconverted are in a desperate condition.

How can these problems be overcome? The Holy Spirit is the answer. When the gospel is preached, the Holy Spirit will convict of sin, reveal Jesus, and draw the unconverted to the cross. This is clear from John's Gospel chapters 14, 15, and 16. In a way in which we do not fully understand, by the working of God's Spirit, the unconverted are given the will and ability to come to Jesus. In fact, there is great responsibility laid upon the unconverted to trust in Jesus; they must repent of sin and believe in Jesus as Savior and Lord.

The Call to Preach

To those unconverted at my own and other churches, the Word of God says, "Blessed are they who keep his testimonies, who seek him with their whole heart." "I love those who love me, and those who seek me diligently find me." "Seek the Lord while he may be found; call on him while he is near." "But seek first the kingdom of God and his righteousness, and all these things will be added to you." "Ask and it will be given to you; seek and you will find; knock and it will be opened to you." "And without faith it is impossible to please Him, for whoever would draw near to God must believe that he exists and that he rewards those who seek him." (Psalm 119:2; Proverbs 8:17; Isaiah 55:6; Matthew 6:33; 7:7; and Hebrews 11:6)

As the gospel is preached, a miraculous drawing occurs.

There is often a great hunger for forgiveness and a desire to be right with God. There may be a great dread of hell and a desire to be safe in Christ. This is the work of the Holy Spirit and a work we should expect when the gospel is preached. As Paul explained, "Faith comes from hearing, and hearing through the word of Christ" (Romans 10:17).

Cornelius' Prayer

When Cornelius, the Roman centurion, sought after the God of Israel, the angel of the Lord said to him: "Your prayers and your alms have ascended as a memorial before God" (Acts 10:4). Though he was yet unconverted, God heard his prayers. Based on this, I urge unconverted people who are seeking Jesus to pray for two things. First, pray that they would see their sin as it truly is; and second, pray that Jesus and his finished work might be clear to them. When a person wishes to pray such prayers, then that to me is evidence of the working of the Holy Spirit.

The Seeker and the seeker

God is the Seeker of those who seek him; it is God alone who initiates the process. He is the great and good Shepherd who seeks for the wandering sheep; he is the one who diligently sweeps the house until the lost coin is found. And, he will find those he is seeking.

Fourteen

I Don't Care Anymore!

"How did it happen, Francisco, that you gave up?" I asked. "I just don't care anymore. What difference does it make anyway? As hard as I try, I keep ending up back here in prison."

A familiar theme

Though I may hear this equally from a John Smith, a Hector Lopez, a Tyrone Jackson, or a Jack Ten Eagles on my visits to San Quentin Prison, it is the cry of despair and resignation. Emanating often from a giant reservoir of anger, directed towards both society and self, it is an attitude that surely condemns a person to a life of pain.

I am acquainted with it myself. After my divorce in which I lost everything – my family, my job, my home, even my car – I felt as if I didn't care what happened to me anymore. It was as if I had entered a black hole. For two solid years I walked around depressed and behaved as though it didn't matter if I lived or died. I am convinced that if the God of the twenty-third Psalm had not walked with me during that time, I would have indeed died, if not literally, then in every other way. But even during the darkest days, I knew I belonged to

Jesus and that he belonged to me. In a way I do not understand, he lifted me up out of the "slimy pit, out of the mud and mire," and set my feet, once again, on the solid rock. So, at the prison, I feel as though I am a beggar telling another beggar that there is hope.

How does it happen?

Sin is mysterious and powerful, and it is something that dwells in us all. Sin separates us from God, and it separates us from others and even ourselves. We end up alone. Even within a loving family we are alone, trapped deep inside ourselves. If we follow our rebellious nature and are not reigned in or rescued by circumstances – family, friends, the law, the school, the church, and so on – the sin will work like a cancer in us, destroying us a little bit at a time. After a while, all can be lost, every dream dashed to pieces, and we don't care anymore. Into the dark cloud we go, and our blindness overwhelms us.

Of course, this does not happen to us all like it did to Francisco, or even to me; most of us do not get to the very bottom. But we may all approach it. Some days simply go wrong. Bad day may be added to bad week and then joined to awful months. It may be illness, financial disaster, extreme family troubles, rejections, losses, major discouragements – with little light at the end of the tunnel. And if there is no strong foundation like there was for me, well, anything might happen.

Never give up!

Forgiveness of sin is a wonderful thing. Knowing that God is real and that he cares for us is a powerful realization. The fact that this world is not our ultimate home brings us great hope and joy. Jesus went to the very end of all things for us, dying in our place. He took the worst there is and did it for us. However bad it gets, Jesus can rescue us and He does it regularly and consistently. To the Franciscos in the dark cloud, I can confidently assure them that, although they have given up on themselves, Jesus has not. He is like that Father who sees his runaway son coming back home and hurries to embrace him; or like the Good Shepherd who walks the dreaded places searching for the lost and wounded sheep. He never gives up, so even if you don't care anymore, you must never give up either.

Fifteen

How It Works

This title is taken from the "big book" of Alcoholics Anonymous, chapter 5, which is sometimes read at their meetings. It explains the basics of the famous "12 Step Program," and because of its simplicity and clarity, it is helpful to new members in particular. Similarly, this chapter intends to express with some simplicity and hopefully some clarity how the Christian life works.

It is a Mystery

How the Christian life works is a mystery. This admission may seem to compromise the goal of simplicity and clarity, even bring it into question altogether, but it must be stated, since it is the truth. How a person, from a human perspective, becomes a Christian in the first place is not easily explained nor completely understood by anyone. The Bible is not laid out in a doctrinally systematic format; rather, we find small portions of hundreds of doctrinal points scattered throughout. But when the key points on salvation are put together, it becomes plain that conversion – the new birth, becoming a Christian, being saved (all synonymous terms) – describe a work that God actually does – spiritually, within, for, and to a person.

Salvation is the one great concern and is therefore the focus of the testimony of both Scripture and Christian doctrine, regardless of denomination. Separated as we are from God, due to sin, only judgment and eternal death await the unconverted. This is the greatest of losses, and God in his love reaches out to us in Christ.

The Outline

The following outline is comprised of two points: salvation and sanctification. It is necessary to use such words; we must not be afraid of them, for they contain the essence of how it works.

Salvation means conversion, or how it is that a person is saved or born again. It encompasses repentance and faith. *Sanctification* describes the spiritual growing up or spiritual maturation of a Christian. This is analogous to the physical birth of a human being and the natural process of growing into physical maturity.

1. Salvation

Before anyone is ever converted, he will hear, or somehow become acquainted with, the basic tenets of the gospel of Jesus Christ, which involve the crucifixion, death, burial and resurrection of Jesus. The gospel message may be communicated through a book, a film, or a personal conversation, but it is usually communicated through preaching. This is clearly depicted in Romans 10:17: "So faith comes from what is heard, and what is heard comes by the preaching of Christ" (RSV).

Faith is a gift from God. "For by grace you have been saved through faith. And this is not your own doing; it is the gift of God, not a result of works, so that no one may boast" (Ephesians 2:8-9). No one has faith apart from it being given by the Holy Spirit. This much is clear. No one can repent unless sin is seen for what it is, and it is the Holy Spirit who reveals this truth. No one has the capacity to repent and believe apart from the influence of God. This is what is meant by grace – God makes it possible to repent and believe, since no one can do it alone or on their own.

It is God's Holy Spirit who reveals to a person that he has sinned against God, who produces a desire to turn from that sin, and then reveals Jesus to be the Savior who is able and willing to forgive all sin. Then the great mystery of conversion occurs. In a way we do not fully understand, a person is "born again." Salvation is completely a work of God. It does not result from a person's good deeds.

Someone might ask at this juncture, "What can I do?" A jailer in the ancient city of Philippi asked this very question of the apostle Paul. The response was, "Believe in the Lord Jesus" (Acts 16:31). The jailer believed right there and then. How did he do it? Well, we are not told exactly how, except that it was by the power of God.

So, then, how can you believe in Jesus? You will believe only by the influence of God's Holy Spirit, which begins with the Spirit of God creating in you the desire to believe in Jesus, just as he did with the Philippian jailer. To go beyond this is to go beyond Scripture itself. The invitation is to repent of your sin and believe in Jesus. Anyone can do this, since the Bible says that whosoever will may come to him. I will add, "Look to Jesus and be saved."

2. Sanctification

Sanctification means to be set aside by God as his own and for his service, and it begins right at the moment of conversion. In fact, each Christian is thoroughly sanctified or made holy by God at the instant of his conversion. This is why Christians are called "saints," a term derived from the word "sanctified." A Christian is a saint and is holy, or sanctified, not because of anything the Christian has done, but solely because of what God has done. God has both placed within every Christian the righteousness of Jesus, and the Christian into Jesus, who is holy and without any blemish or sin. This is not an easy concept to grasp, but it is thoroughly biblical.

Although the Christian is sanctified and is considered completely holy by God, he still continues to sin. This is indeed paradoxical, but again, it is what the Scripture teaches. This has been the experience of Christians right from the beginning. We have been born anew by the Spirit of God, and we have been given the gift of eternal life, yet we find ourselves sinning.

Not that the Christian is to continue in sin as a way of life. No, we are to turn away from sin and seek to honor and please God. But there is within us the mystery of sin, something incredibly powerful that will sometimes gain certain victories over us. Nevertheless, despite our sin, the sureness of our salvation is never in question. Our salvation depends on what God has done in Christ and not upon our ability or strength to refrain from sinning.

Sanctification is a process that continues throughout our lifetime. We go forward little by little; sometimes we even seem to be going backwards. Paul put it this way: "...work out your own salvation with fear and trembling, for it is God who works in you, both to will and to work for his good pleasure" (Philippians 2:12-13). Paul urges the Christian to "work out your own salvation" while at the same time asserting that God is at work in the life of the Christian to do that very thing. It is a paradox. We cling to both of these truths simultaneously.

Assurance and Peace

In reality, it works as we trust in Jesus. This is it in a nutshell; but everything is centered on the fact that Jesus has secured our salvation and sanctification.

Jesus is the source of our assurance and peace. We have eternal life right now, and God is continually working with us, bringing us to maturity in Christ.

Sixteen

How We Know We Are Christians

"Am I a Christian?" Since no certificate of authentication comes to us from the hand of God upon conversion, the answer to this critical question must ultimately be an experience of faith.

It is one thing to claim salvation, as though one could, but it is quite another to know one has been claimed. However, we can have clear indications that we are. It is much like the evidence that proves we are human beings. Humans look like, act like, and think like homosapiens and not like other species. Jesus' characterization of conversion as a spiritual new birth was neither random nor careless; it was a deliberate analogy. As there are traits associated with humanness, so too are there traits associated with being a born-again Christian. It is on the basis of the presence of these spiritual traits that we can know by faith that we are indeed Christians.

The rest of this essay is divided into two sections. The first section concerns those experiences that normally come before conversion, and the second section outlines those experiences that normally, but not always, come after conversion. These are set in a particular order in terms of spiritual experiences, but this should not be relied upon. Experiences will, of course, differ to some degree from person to person. In addition, one should not be too particular in matching his or her experience with those given here. Since each person is different, considerable variation can be expected in how the Holy Spirit works with the individual. However, there is a common core of spiritual experiences that come to most people.

The following points have either been experienced by me, someone I know, or someone I have read about.

Before Conversion, there may be...
- A sense of meaninglessness or purposelessness. Some have described it as a spiritual or emotional restlessness. It may be intense and last for a long period of time. Or, it may be mild and of short duration, but all the while life seems somewhat disjointed and uneasy.
- A desire that the grave is not the end of life. Some have had a sense of anger that life could be so short and harsh. "There must be more than this" expresses the hope for life after death. This is not so much a fear of death as it is a love of life.
- A sense that there will be a judgment. This was my experience, and I could not account for it.
- A sense of being lost and alone, abandoned and orphaned. This most unpleasant feeling troubles us persistently and will not let us go.
- Anger and confusion, even anxiety, at being so vulnerable and out of control. Friends might suggest therapy at such a time, but if the advice is followed, it provides no real relief.
- A sense of unworthiness, of having done wrong, of feeling guilty, even of being ashamed. This sense of ourselves persists even though we affirm philosophies that are rel-

ativistic and have no moral content.
- A sharp, even painful realization of having broken God's holy laws and thus standing condemned before him. This is a major step beyond the previous experience. Here there is a clear and unmistakable recognition that God is real and that we are lawbreakers.
- A sense of being spiritually naked, wretched, and miserable. This, again, is a step beyond the previous experience and is most uncomfortable. It is somewhat rare in the conversion experiences I have read, but not absent completely, as the testimonies of George Whitefield and John Bunyan reveal.
- Perhaps a period of trying to be self-righteous. We attempt to strike a balance between sins and good actions. Performing good deeds produces a temporary sense of well-being, which is followed by failures that produce a sense of personal disgust.
- A goal to be a "good person." There may be sensitivity, almost of a paranoid nature, that others, particularly Christians, are judging us and thinking we are not good people.
- Serious attempts at severe religiosity, even involving material self-denial. This is rare but not unheard of.
- Giving up on the attempt to become acceptable to God. Some resign themselves to a hopeless condition and fear they will never be good enough to receive forgiveness.
- A sense, sometimes accompanied by an inner desperation, of having a hardened heart and a callous mind. Some may even feel out of touch with reality.
- Efforts to understand the Bible and actually get to the bottom of what Christianity is all about.
- An interest in Jesus beginning to take form. Out of fear of being ridiculed, we keep this interest a secret. Some, however, are aggressive in their seeking and don't care

who knows or what they think.
- An exposure, in some manner or another, to the gospel. It may be via hearing preaching, a personal conversation, a book or other printed material, a song, a radio or television preacher, a film, even a conversation overheard at a coffee shop.
- Now, the Holy Spirit drawing or calling us to Christ. Little else matters now. Only two things are clear: our own sinfulness and the forgiveness that is in Jesus.
- A sense that Jesus himself is calling out to us.
- The hearing of his voice and knowing that nothing can keep us from him.
- Now the extreme irresistibility of Jesus as he calls us to himself.

At this point, conversion (the new birth) occurs. We do not know how or what or why, but there is newness. It may happen quietly or with great emotion or something in-between.

After Conversion
- Some are immediately joyful and have a sense of being at rest.
- Some feel as though a great burden has been lifted from their shoulders.
- Some feel nothing at all.
- Some, like I was, are confused initially. Yet the inner spiritual conflict has ended.
- Some are fearful as to what the change in them will bring. I was worried that I would lose friends. My mother's reaction was a major concern, as I knew she was antagonistic towards Christianity.
- Some will experience rejection from family and friends.
- Some will have a great desire, which is very unusual for them, to read the Bible. This was certainly true for me, as

I could not find enough time to read it.
- Some will want to be with other Christians, even attend church and worship. At first, the newness and strangeness associated with worship and hymn singing may be uncomfortable, but the "baby" Christian knows where he will be nurtured.
- Some will be drawn to prayer and will spend long periods praying to God. The sudden realization that God is real, that he loves and cares for us, that there is an actual reason for existence is quite overwhelming, and we love to fellowship with God.
- Some will, and usually fearfully, attempt to tell others what happened to them.
- Some will decide to keep it all a secret, especially after they are rebuffed by significant people in their lives due to their testimony.
- Some will want to join a Bible study to learn all they possible can about Jesus and the Bible. Though everything that is said and taught is not quickly understood, there will be persistence in "growing in the Word."
- There may be an initial period of euphoria, but this will end and things will seem, emotionally speaking, much as they were before the conversion.
- Sin may become an issue. Some will have the sense that they are hopeless sinners, some will be mad that so much of their life was sin-oriented, and some will think they are not good enough to be Christians. This last one was true of me. Not understanding that sanctification was a lifelong process and that I had already been declared righteous in Christ, I seriously thought about dropping out altogether.
- Some will end one sin only to find another one to deal with. Occasionally a new Christian will feel hopeless, only to discover that they are not righteous at all and that

only Jesus is.
- There is a continuing desire to turn away from sin.
- Identifying with Jesus and other Christians, even when it means censor or rejection from others, comes to characterize us. For me, this meant ostracism from some friends and co-workers.
- There is a desire for water baptism.
- There is a desire to receive the Lord's Supper.
- There is a desire to be of service and to be faithful with material possessions. I experienced this about six months after my conversion. At first, I sang in the choir and put just a minimal amount into the offering plate. Before long, I was teaching a junior high Sunday school class and tithing my money.
- A desire to please and honor God. This becomes a continuing desire and lifelong expression of our love for God.
- A continuing sense of our own unworthiness.
- A continuing dependency on Jesus and his righteousness.
- A delight in hearing the gospel preached; hearing a good sermon becomes more important than going to a sporting or musical event.
- Sunday becomes a special day for worship, ministry, and rest.
- We feel constrained to give up a "habit" that we have come to believe is not pleasing to God.
- Being faithful with money even when funds are running short.
- Appreciation for and love of hymn lyrics such as:
  "Amazing grace! How sweet the sound that saved a wretch like me!"
  "There is a fountain filled with blood"
  "My Jesus, I love Thee"
  "For Thee all the follies of sin I resign"
  "Tell me the story of Jesus, Write on my heart every

word"

"Fairest Lord Jesus! Thee will I honor, Thou, my soul's Glory, Joy, and Crown!"

"O for a thousand tongues to sing my great Redeemer's praise."

"Jesus, the very thought of Thee with sweetness fills my breast."

"My richest gain I count but loss, and pour contempt on all my pride."

"So I'll cherish the old rugged cross."

"Would He devote that sacred head for such a worm as I"

(It would have been impossible for me to sing words such as these before my conversion; and, it took a while to get used to them, but once I did, I loved them).

- A determination to follow Jesus despite doubts. A settled and fixed theology does not come with conversion. Early on I thought everything I heard from the pulpit and from my new Christian friends was absolute truth. Later, I had to make each and every point of doctrine my own. This is not easily or quickly done.
- If a major failure occurs, even a moral scandal, the person of faith will still, eventually, continue to trust in Jesus. I have had my problems, but by God's grace he did not abandon me or correct me so harshly that I gave up on myself.
- Even in the midst of mental, theological, and emotional confusion there is a determination to love and follow Jesus, though we should be cast into hell. I noticed that some of the English and American Puritans spoke like this and it took me some time to understand that they were expressing their fallibility while upholding God's sovereignty.
- A desire that our life should glorify God.

- A desire that our death should glorify God.
- A desire that at the judgment of Christ we would hear him say to us, "Well done, good and faithful servant. Enter into the joy of your rest."

Part Two

Eighteen Essays

Seventeen

If It's Organized Religion, It Must Be Bad

"What else would you expect from organized religion!"

Notice the exclamation point. My Word program expected a question mark, but no, the person who disagreed with something I said in a YouTube video dismissed what I said by identifying me with "organized religion." So was born this little essay.

Granted, organized religion, including Christianity, is a minefield, and that's a statement from someone who has been a pastor for over forty-four years. I have myself been blown up a few times and have been responsible for taking others with me. I guess I could complain and look for someone to blame, but that would gain nothing.

Wherever two or more are gathered together, there is bound to be trouble.

And why is this? One sinner alone is bad enough, two or more is worse, as there is suddenly more sin all in one place.

Is there a church in the New Testament that was without fault? Maybe the church at Smyrna or Philadelphia (see Revelation 2:8-11 and 3:7-13), yet even the very early church in

Jerusalem had its troubles.

Long ago, after being completely rejected from a church, I decided to leave organized churches all together and explore home churches. Without going into detail, that failed too, and I was going to give up again. At that point I came to a realization that my idealizing of the very concept of church was at the core of my problem. I was shocked when things went wrong; I should have been shocked when things went right! Are not the devil and the demons hot after the churches? Smear a church, a pastor, an elder, a deacon, and so on, and what a victory for the dark side. It might even make the papers or the alphabet news at prime time.

Some folks have been so burned by churches, and we are talking here about church leaders as well as congregants, that even the thought of church, even hearing the word, is enough to nauseate them. But what is the alternative?

What religion is in question here?

The responder to the YouTube had Christianity in mind, for sure. Yes, we Christians are organized and have been for quite a long time. We have our churches, pre-schools, high schools, colleges, universities, hospitals, grand cathedrals, publishing houses, charitable organizations, creeds, statements of faith, doctrines, theologies, traditions, and leaders. Whether Roman Catholic, Eastern Orthodox, Protestant, or whatever, what we believe and practice is open and evident to all. Is chaotic and disorganized a better way to operate?

In fact, all the world's religions are organized, and some on a par with or more so than Christianity. Buddhism is highly organized and regulated; Judaism, certainly; and Islam, extremely so. Name one that is not organized; it is probably without even a name.

What about neo-paganistic religions like Wicca? Also highly organized, including how to go at it solo; even shamanistic groups are sophisticated and well defined. No, they are all organized, and if one isn't, it simply fades away.

I think I know what was bothering the person who responded to me. It was clear I belong to organized religion, and she felt uncomfortable with me, and as a result thought I was defending the "establishment" at all costs and so could not be trusted. I was a company man, only interested in the bottom line. Perhaps that is it. I reasoned in that way at one time in my life. But Christianity is an individual thing; each Christian walks his or her own walk.

Christianity is the focus

The YouTube viewer was also angered at a stance I took on homosexuality, but it could have been any number of issues. As a Christian, I have points of view and am not ashamed to express them. I do not expect everyone to agree with me; in fact, I would be surprised if even a sizable minority did. The Scripture, both Old and New Testaments, express a morality that is rejected by a growing majority. I know this, but I do not feel compelled to go along to get along. The morals and ethics of the Bible have stood the test of time and have been shown to be reliable, trustworthy, and beneficial. I may not always agree and may have quibbles with some things, but overall, I will go with the Word of the Creator rather than what fallen human beings invent.

Seeing this does not come easily, because most of us come kicking and screaming into finally recognizing truth, since we all have been disobedient and rebellious. We bristle at biblical statements about being blinded by sin and the devil and about our hearts being deceitful above all things, so we reject truth and cling to the dictates of our flesh and whatever ethics happen to be popular. Yes, we tend to be God-haters and mockers, leveling insults at Christians, since God is not handy and available for a good rant or vent. As a high school student I loved to point out the faults of the Christian kids I knew. Not only was I prideful and judgmental, but I completely overestimated how wonderful I was. Hypocrite is a word that comes to mind.

Organized? Holy? Pure?

No institution that humans develop is perfectly structured and without error. Christians are only somewhat successful at organizing. No Christian is holy and pure, either. Growing up to be like Jesus is a life-long process that we approach little by little. We know this is how it is with us. Who is perfect? None, no, not one. Our strange and unholy ways corrupt everything we touch. We must be careful not to become complacent or be tempted to turn a blind eye toward that which is ungodly. No, we cling the closer to the revealed truth and stand by it even to our detriment. The Church is always and constantly in need of revival.

Non-Religious organizations

This past week a psychiatrist was sent to prison for many years for molesting boys he counseled at a juvenile facility. A dentist in a town near me had an affair with a client and ended up murdering the woman's husband. A general practitioner developed an addiction to gambling and inexpertly juggled the books to cover her losses. A judge was removed from office for corruption. A bunch of cops in a famous city nearby got caught stealing drugs out of the evidence room. And on and on it goes, and I will not even bother to bring up situations involving nationally known celebrities and politicians.

Now then, do we throw all the institutions and organizations represented by the above list of miscreants under the bus? Of course not. We are reality-oriented, and we know that people will take advantage of power positions and do crazy things. This is true for every human association, including churches. Could it be any different?

Concluding thought

Was the responder to my YouTube video claiming to be standing on higher ground than the organized religionists? Probably not, so what was the point? Let me offer a suggestion.

When we run into a holy God and a holy morality, we shudder and shake inwardly because of the embedded truth in our conscience, whether we recognize the process or not. We cannot easily get away from it. We cope by clinging to a philosophy that is pliable enough to accommodate whatever it is we happen to believe in or be involved in. The Bible draws lines, and we are left then with either trying to erase them or going into denial all together. I have sometimes wondered if a lot of substance abuse is not involved here; conscious self-disapproving thoughts must be squashed.

Organized religion is often bad, and we know this now. So, the people or group that is organized or even disorganized but is not religious is the one we can depend upon to tell the truth and do right. Right? Okay, I get it now.

Eighteen

Strikes and Outs

"Strikes and Outs" – baseball lingo – but this essay is not about baseball; it is about courage.

Strikes and outs are what umpires, those who officiate baseball games, are supposed to call. A "call" is when an umpire indicates that a pitched ball is either a ball or a strike or that a runner is safe or out. Batters do not want to hear a pitched ball called a strike, and the umpire knows this well. Runners hate being called out. It takes courage to call strikes and outs.

Then consider a "play" as when a runner is coming into home plate and arrives at about the same time as a ball thrown by a fielder. A call of safe or out must be made, and it is easier to make the safe call – any seasoned umpire will say amen to that. Unless, of course, the call is clearly wrong, in which case confusion ensues.

How do I know this? I have umpired many games, and most of them were played at San Quentin State Prison. The strikes and outs are not good news to the convicts when they're called against the home team, and all the convicts' games are home games. One contested call may mean that an ump will be heckled by a disgruntled fan or player for the entire game.

In the last game of our season at the prison we needed an umpire, since our usual ump had just paroled. I volunteered, and during the course of the game the subject for this essay came to mind.

As it is easier to signal that a pitch is a ball or to make a safe call, so it is easier to stand down and avoid confronting error. Courage is a rare and wonderful quality, one which may cost us dearly.

A price paid for obedience

We see in the pages of the New Testament the price Jesus paid for His obedience to the Father. He was attacked by many, scorned and rejected, and ultimately went to the cross. His Passion was the express will of God, yet we see the tortuous process that went with standing for the truth.

Paul would have understood my baseball analogy – he called strikes and outs and paid the price for it. He took stands for the Gospel that earned him enemies and a stressful life.

John was opposed by the Roman authorities and was forced into exile, yet he never ceased to speak out against error nor shrunk from lifting up Jesus as Lord, even in the face of severe and murderous emperor worship.

The Church has had its heroes, men and women of faith and vision, who have been defenders of the Faith delivered once and for all to the Church. Christians in whatever era are called to do the same. And it takes courage to do so.

Taking a stand against error

Currently I am in a struggle or two and am discovering again what it is to take a stand. It is even more difficult, if the stand is against error within the broad Christian community. Many do not understand that spiritual warfare is waged more often inside the "visible" church than outside it. The secular world is one thing, but issues of biblical doctrine and practice impact us more directly and critically than the ongoing confusion in the world.

Fewer topics arouse my reaction these days, and for this I am thankful. One of my life goals is to avoid giving in to a cynical, complaining attitude, always looking for what is wrong rather than what is right. There are far too many issues abroad that can get me stirred up, so I must be selective and focus only on those things that go to the heart of the biblical and evangelical Gospel. I cannot be afraid to call strikes and outs.

The biblical warnings and warrants

Here are passages I look to in order to remind myself that certain error must be opposed, regardless of the probability of negative reactions.

> ***Matthew 24:4-5***: "See that no one leads you astray. For many will come in my name, saying, 'I am the Christ.' And they will lead many astray."

Jesus' words to His apostles were meant for something more than information, I would think. Perhaps they were to be actively opposing those who announced they were the Messiah. Such pretenders may or may not have come from within the Christian community, but from wherever the false claim originated, there would be an evil harvest.

> ***Acts 20:28-31a:*** "Pay careful attention to yourselves and to all the flock, in which the Holy Spirit has made your overseers, to care for the church of God, which he obtained with his own blood. I know that after my departure fierce wolves will come in among you, not

sparing the flock; and from among your own selves will arise men speaking twisted things, to draw away the disciples after them. Therefore be alert."

Paul delivered this warning to the elders of the Church at Ephesus, and it is reasonable to expect that the current elders of God's Flock must heed the same warning. Notice the emphasis here: the trouble will come from within, not outside the church, which is so often the case. Over four decades of ministry, my experience has been that opposition from outside the church is less common; it is nearly always from within the visible church that the trouble arises.

Galatians 1:6-9: "I am astonished that you are so quickly deserting him who called you in the grace of Christ and are turning to a different gospel—not that there is another one, but there are some who trouble you and want to distort the gospel of Christ. But even if we or an angel from heaven should preach to you a gospel contrary to the one we preached to you, let him be accursed. As we have said before, so now I say again: If anyone is preaching to you a gospel contrary to the one you received, let him be accursed."

"Accursed" – precisely what Paul had in mind in using such a word is unknown, but at minimum accursed is not a good thing. Paul is courageous in his concern for the Galatian churches and speaks his mind. Though he might anticipate that his direct warning will stir up trouble, he writes because he is aware of the greater problems that would result if a false gospel were to make its way into those churches. Paul again warns that the platform for the presentation of the strange gospel would be from within the Christian community.

Beware of angelic revelations

Paul may not be going to an extreme when he mentions a gospel coming from an angel. More than once persons have claimed angelic revelation. One only has to think of Islam and Mormonism for illustrations. As crazy as it seems, angels or what present themselves as angels, are up to the same old tricks right now. Fallen angels–demons--are spiritual and powerful ("angels of light" Paul called them--see 2 Corinthians 11:14), and it is very hard to resist that which seems to come from God.

> ***1 Timothy 4:1:*** "Now the Spirit expressly says that in later times some will depart from the faith by devoting themselves to deceitful spirits and teachings of demons."

Whether these days are the last days or not is unknown, but they may be, and so the warning of Paul could easily be applicable. Those who will be devoting themselves to the demons have departed from "the faith." Again the trouble arises from within the visible church. And it is not mentioned if the devotees are genuine Christians or are unbelievers supposing themselves to be born again but are merely *christianized.* [1]

Could it be that we have been living in the "later times" for a long time, perhaps even from the time of Jesus' earthly ministry? (see 1 John 2:18). A survey of the history of our

---

1   By "christianized" I mean someone who has all the appearances of being a Christian, yet is not actually born again. False conversion may be fairly common when it is thought that by repeating a prayer, coming forward at an altar call, engaging in what are thought to be spiritual gifts, submitting to an organization's requirements for membership, confessing and adhering to doctrinal positions, or doing anything within human capacity, one automatically becomes a Christian.

Church might lend support to the concept.

> **1 John 4:1:** "Beloved, do not believe every spirit, but test the spirits to see whether they are from God, for many false prophets have gone out into the world."

Upsetting indeed – "many false prophets" going out into the world, so the Apostle John sounds the warning. Is the same occurring today?

> **Jude 3-4:** "Beloved, although I was very eager to write to you about our common salvation, I found it necessary to write appealing to you to contend for the faith that was once for all delivered to the saints. For certain people have crept in unnoticed who long ago were designated for this condemnation, ungodly people, who pervert the grace of our God into sensuality and deny our only Master and Lord, Jesus Christ."

Jude would rather have written a celebratory letter focused on the grace and mercy of the Lord Jesus but of necessity had to urge the readers to "contend for the faith." And it has always been so.

Once again, the trouble comes from people who have made their way into the Christian churches. Here the problem might have been easy to spot, due to the blatant sinfulness of those who would pervert the Gospel. How it was that these were "designated for this condemnation" is not apparent. However, the message is simple: strange and false doctrine will be proclaimed, and it must be understood for what it is and withstood.

Be strong and courageous

Before long I will be an old man, but I was once a young

lion ready to take on any foe. It is more taxing for me now and more stressful to listen to the heckling when strikes and outs are called. It is now apparent that I need my community of faith, the congregation I pastor, to stand alongside me.

A passage I memorized some decades ago gives me continued strength to stand and deliver:

> ***Joshua 1:9:*** "Have I not commanded you? Be strong and courageous. Do not be frightened, and do not be dismayed, for the LORD your God is with you wherever you go."

Nineteen

We Are Hypocrites, You Know

I admit to being one – a hypocrite that is – and you are probably one, too.

I've heard it before. "Philpott, you are a hypocrite. Look at your life; you have practically made shipwreck of it. Don't you dare criticize me!"

That lovely comment came immediately after I expressed an opinion to an individual, based on his confession, that it might be better to stop stealing from the his employer. My hands were not clean; after all, I am a divorced and remarried pastor, so I had no standing to "judge" anyone.

Why is this so? And, am I any different than other Christians? We are all called to the highest standard: to love God with all we are and love our neighbors as ourselves. John, the Gospel writer, was convinced of the fact that we will continue to sin, and he wrote specifically to Christians, "If we say we have not sinned, we make him a liar, and his word in not in us" (1 John 1:10). He went on to give Christians of all ages a sweet word of relief: "My little children, I am writing these things to you so that you may not sin. But if anyone does sin, we have an advocate with the Father, Jesus Christ the righteous" (1 John 2:1).

It is interesting to note than John assumes we will sin. This is evident in his use of what grammarians refer to as a third class conditional clause carried in the "if" at the beginning of the verse 10 in chapter 1. It means that the Christians to whom he is writing probably, even likely, will sin.

That we were sinners before we knew Christ is easily accepted. But dealing with our own sin after conversion and maybe while a leader in a local church does not come so simply.

Anyone of us with the slightest self-awareness knows we still sin, even those who claim to be Spirit-filled and "moving in the power," and there is little sense in denying our reality. One thing we must do is to be honest with ourselves, but the Pharisee in us has trouble with this. Somehow we think if we admit sin then we must be worthless, maybe are not even saved. So we lie to ourselves and resort to lies, comparing ourselves with others who are obviously terrible, awful, bad sinners – people like me.

We are so often tempted to play the role of Pharisee, aren't we? In Matthew chapter 23 are the seven woes. Jesus said to those who thought of themselves as faithful law keepers, "Woe to you." We may think we are imitating Him when we point the finger at others, but it is often nothing more than a case of knowing another's sins and using this against them. Our behavior is not righteous; it is deflection and certainly not graceful or merciful.

I am almost used to hearing it. "Philpott, you are no good. How can you stand up there and preach? What a hypocrite; you have broken practically all the commandments. No, you have broken them all and worse."

I can only plead guilty.

What am I to do with this? Maybe I should just stand down and keep my mouth shut, find a cave in the desert, crawl in, and die. And shockingly, there are those who would like to see me do exactly that. When I went to law school I learned you have to have clean hands to go to court. My hands are dirty, and there is nothing I can do about it now. I have repented more than most people my age, and it looks like I will have to continue until I drop dead. It is a full time job.

Yes, I admit I am rightfully accused much of the time, but I have been washed, sanctified, and justified, all by means of the shed blood of Jesus Christ (see 1 Corinthians 6:9). His cleansing blood has atoned for and covered all of my sin – past, present, and future. He therefore gives me the confidence and courage to continue in the servant work I am privileged to do.

But there is someone else who accuses me, and he never lets up. Even if I could uproot myself, change my name, and get a complete face-lift, the devil would still follow me to the ends of the earth and attack me mercilessly.

Satan is the "accuser of our brothers" (Revelation 12:10). He attempts to undermine our peace and assurance by dredging up our past failures. Satan likes to make us feel that we are so bad we might as well quit. It is one of his favorite lies he whispers to Christians. And how does this cruel enemy do this? The short answer is, through others, people close to us, and very often who are in the Faith.

Now, not everyone has made "shipwreck" of their faith and bungled things to a severe extent, but even these extreme cases need not give up and follow the devil. Therefore, even if I went off the deep end while I was a Christian, I should tell the devil to go to his assigned place, hell.

Grace is grace, and though it is not a license to sin, there is restoration, reconciliation, and more work in the vineyard. We go on following Jesus, aware that we are damaged goods, yet the Holy – emphasize *Holy* – Spirit dwells in us, and our names are written forever in the Lamb's Book of Life (see

Revelation 21:27). With that in mind, we go on with a combination of courage and humility.

The devil can rage, and the Pharisees among us can criticize and castigate, but we do not listen to these voices. We are sheep who know the Shepherd's voice, and we stumble along after Him.

Twenty

Feeling the Spirit?

I was once a wild-eyed Pentecostal. Before that I was a rock 'n roller, feeling the beat, the louder the better. Detractors – those non-spiritual Christians who surely did not even have the Spirit at all, warned that the people at the church I pastored were experiencing something emotion-based and not from the Holy Spirit. I would laugh at the sour grape nay-sayers, the wannabes who would dance to the praise and worship band if only they had one. I felt sorry for them as I imagined their dead, cold services.

Somewhere, somehow I changed my mind. It may have been the day I woke up to the fact that I needed more and more music, swaying, waving of arms, and singing repetitiously the same chorus to get to that happy place where I could say, "The Holy Spirit has shown up."

The church I now pastor is home to a few folks who have come from charismatic or Pentecostal churches. At times they have pressed me to get more excitement into the worship services. Despite my stories of my days as a Spirit-filled rocking pastor, I could see that my explanation was not working. They could not see anything wrong with feeling the Spirit – after all, didn't God make our emotions, too? And this one really hurt: if I was really evangelistic as I claimed, it would not matter how we got the butts into the pews, just as long as we did.

They further maintained, what was the harm of having some good feeling going on at church? Of course, I can get just as easily get worked up singing the Gloria Patri, even the old standard Doxology, but young people need more, the argument goes. The new generation is unlike any other, and they respond only to cutting edge techy media stuff.

There are going to be feelings and emotions, happiness and tears, and sometimes more than that in a worship service. These cannot be avoided and neither should they be. But, and this is the point I want to make, to equate the Holy Spirit with feelings is dead wrong.

Looking at the early Church

Acts 2:42 provides a glimpse of the day by day practice of the early church. "And they devoted themselves to the apostles' teaching and fellowship, to the breaking of bread and the prayers." And this is presented in the same chapter as the Day of Pentecost events and Peter's first sermon. There is not a word about music, yet in that era there were musical instruments and choirs in abundance, since it was common practice in the Temple worship to have both. Let me be clear that I am not against choirs and music – we have both in the church I pastor; in fact, I play choruses each Sunday on my guitar and am accompanied by a bass guitar, piano, a mandolin, and a drum. But it fits into the worship service, during a short time, and it is not done in such a way as to produce a sense that the Spirit has now arrived. None of it is designed to produce an emotionally charged environment that must occur as the "praise choruses" are sung on and on to a captivating and interesting beat.

Of the five "pentecosts" in Acts – two in Jerusalem (Acts

2 and 4), one in Samaria (Acts 8), another in Caesarea (Acts 10), and yet another in Ephesus (Acts 19), there is not one mention of any form of music. No, the message of Jesus was proclaimed and the Holy Spirit came in power to save. In fact, nowhere in the book of Acts is there any mention of music, much less a praise band and swaying to any beat at all.

Paul mentions twice in his letters the singing of psalms, hymns, and spiritual songs (see Ephesians 5:19 and Colossians 3:16). For a Jewish man accustomed to Levitical worship his statements make perfect sense. This is a far cry from what goes on in the churches where music dominates the worship and moves people into a feeling, emotion-centered activity, that often morphs into what are thought to be charismatic gifts of the Spirit.

I spoke in tongues for years and introduced it to thousands of people in the 1970s. I have heard thousands speak in tongues in large meetings and in small prayer meetings. For many years I led people into prolonged singing of praise choruses until the singing in the spirit, the prophesying, and other more strange things, including wild dancing, began to take place. Always we thought it was solely due to the Spirit showing up. None of these things would occur during the preaching and teaching of the Bible and the Gospel, events which were fairly mild and calm. The idea was generated that the Bible preaching and teaching was only a run-up to the real thing. This mistake led us to greater and greater error.

The appearance of evangelistic success

Filling up a place with people is not the same as God's calling, justifying, and glorifying (see Romans 8:30). An influx of people into a church building may or may not be the result of genuine conversions. During the Jesus People Movement, roughly 1967 to 1975, those who were being saved came as regular as clock work. But once that wonderful awakening was concluded by God's sovereign hand, the conversions were slower, really few and far between. Not understanding how God works, we manufactured attraction, and it was primarily through music. To a degree, it worked or appeared to work, but it was different. We had to get professional, practiced, and careful in the creation of a worshipful ambience – but it was planning and process. We became entertainers meeting felt needs, and we created networks of people so that social bonding would take place. We developed small groups that were designed to connect people. The pews and chairs were occupied, and we called it evangelism.

There was, however, something else that took place, and even now I am shocked at the unbiblical nature of it: We assumed that everyone who praised and worshiped with speaking "in the Spirit" had to be born again, since we were convinced that the exercise of such a biblical gift was sure indication of the indwelling of the Holy Spirit. That became our evangelism. There was virtually no need to preach the message of the cross; all we needed was a good praise and worship team. Some of us at that time detected, to a degree, that something was wrong. Our efforts to move many of these people into Bible study groups were not successful. What people wanted was the music and the bliss of zoning out.

Let me confess that it took two decades to see my error. I wanted so badly to succeed and be well known and admired. In addition, I had a family to provide for. What was I to do but go along with the dominant model? Then about 1995 I began to change. This was most evident in the plain and simple Gospel messages I began to preach. While there were a few conversions, they did not make up for the numbers of people who went elsewhere. Many a time I considered going back to the old processes. With all I was reading and hearing, it seemed I was out of step, an old fogy, someone trapped in a time warp. In a way I cannot understand, and certainly my emotions had nothing to do with it, I was content with presenting the Word to those who would listen. In describing myself I began to say, "I am an old time Gospel preacher."

An outrageous statement?

There is not one shred of truth to the idea that the Holy Spirit's work is to make us feel good. To put it another way, having feelings in a worship service or some other venue is not the direct action of the Holy Spirit. The objective is to worship the God of our salvation; it is not to have an experience.

There is no supporting biblical evidence that the bodily or physical senses are to be gratified during worship. Someone will say, "Well, what about joy? But joy is a state of mind, the sure knowledge that Jesus has rescued, forgiven, sealed, and indwelt the former dirty rotten sinner headed for hell. The Holy Spirit blesses us also, but there is no evidence that such a blessing is feeling-oriented. I am blessed whether I feel it or not.

My contention is that it is not the Holy Spirit who produces feelings. Feelings may be there or not be there; in either case it has nothing to do with the Spirit of God.

Let me take it one step further. It is misrepresenting the Holy Spirit to equate His presence with feelings. Such may not fall into the category of blaspheming the Spirit, but it is error nevertheless.

Payback

Not that I think that there is anything like cosmic payback, but what I used to dish out to local pastors and churches – "We have the Spirit and you do not" – I am now receiving from young pastors of new church plants: Philpott? Well, all he does is teach the Bible. He needs the Spirit, but he doesn't even have a real band!

There is an old saying that goes something like this:
"Too much Word with too little Spirit, you dry up.
Too much Spirit with too little Word, you blow up.
With the right balance, we grow up."

That may not be exactly the way it goes, but we promoted the idea associated with it during the 1970s to essentially say that we had the right balance and others did not. Too much Word meant that the Holy Spirit was being ignored. Not us, since we had praise and worship with spiritual gifting for at least a half hour at each service. Of course, we assumed that what we were doing was of God. There was no proof of it; there was nothing in Scripture that would validate what we experienced. We took it for granted we were safe, because we learned it from well known and recognized leaders in charismatic/Pentecostal circles. How could we be wrong?

"Right balance." How would one know when a right balance was reached? Is there any biblical passage that would serve as a gauge? Upon further consideration this little piece of sophistry is nothing more than a boast – a sectarian, if not cultic, way of saying we have it and you don't.

A possible response

As a pastor I am troubled by the emphasis on feeling the Spirit. New churches continually show up in our county touting their music ministry and the power of the Spirit in their midst. It gives me the sense that there are wolves circling the sheep in the little flock under my oversight. In doing my job of protecting the flock I have lost a few battles. To two generations now heavily impacted by rock 'n roll, the band sounds awfully good, and the old hymns seem hum-drum, old, and hard to understand with all the Bible doctrine intertwined therein.

What can I do? By His grace I hope to keep doing what

I know is right to do and preach the Word and trust that the Spirit of God is with us. Remember Jesus' promise, "For where two or three are gathered together in my name, there am I among them" (Matthew 18:20).

Finally, it is clear that what the mature believer wants is the meat of the Word and the joyful truth of the Gospel of grace. Faithful pastors and churches must not yield to what looks now to be successful and popular. We have learned that the desire to feel the Spirit becomes insatiable, just like the need for more and more miracles, and thus we are led farther and farther from the clear practice of the early Church.

Beware the feel of the beat and the flesh.

Twenty-One

Christian Moralistic Therapeutic Deism

Mark Galli, former Senior Managing Editor for *Christianity Today*, wrote an article for their October, 2009, edition entitled "In the beginning, grace."

Mr. Galli calls sharp attention to the rapid decline of evangelical Christianity in America as described by a number of different analysts. Apparently the church growth movement and the Christian entertainment industry have turned out, as many thought, to be merely human engineering and not the work of a sovereign God. (British Christians are ahead of American in this regard, since the decline in genuine Christianity has been visible for some time in the UK.) In language not too distant from what I discussed in *Are You Really Born Again?*[1] published by Evangelical Press, part of the problem is that there are those who find themselves identifying with Christian churches who may not actually be born again. (Does this sound judgmental?)

A key element in Mr. Galli's article is based on a study conducted by Christian Smith and Melinda Lundquist Denton. The findings were published in 2005 in a document enti-

---

1 The most recent edition of this book is entitled *A Matter of Life and Death: Understanding True and False Conversion*.

tled *Soul Searching: The Religious and Spiritual Lives of American Teenagers*. In that reporting a term is used to describe the spiritual condition of a majority of the 267 teenagers who made up the sample for the study – Christian Moralistic Therapeutic Deism.

> **Christian**: brought up in a Christian tradition to some degree.
> **Moralistic**: emphasis on doing right and avoidance of doing wrong.
> **Therapeutic**: emphasis on meeting physical and emotional needs.
> **Deism**: no real personal relationship with the living God.

As I contemplated the shocking estimation by Mr. Galli – a person who, in my thinking, has his finger accurately on the spiritual pulse of American Christianity – I began to focus on the four words listed above. Now, some days have passed since my first reading of the article, and after a number of discussions with those whose opinions I value, I have arrived at a few thoughts about what I see in the Christian community I know. Admittedly, I have branched off from the thrust of the Christianity Today article, yet the diversion might be of some value.

Christian – there is much confusion here, I have found. At the risk of being considered judgmental, I assume that anyone who has pastored a church for ten or more years and has been involved in a local Christianity community knows exactly what I am saying and meaning. Knowing doctrine, even Calvinistic doctrine, thoroughly and even solidly holding to the five points, does not guarantee the new birth. Church membership, active Christian service, a devoted life, at least as viewed from the exterior, a good reputation from respected sources, and more – these things are doable and may be sincere but may be entirely false evidence of conversion to Christ. One of my favorite expressions is: "You cannot join Christianity; you must be joined to Christ."

Moralistic – here the focus is on doing right action as a Christian. I have found we are obsessed with what others do or don't do. The apostle Peter might have suffered terribly at the hands of some of those within our Christian communities had they gotten a chance at him. Often I am fearful of what new born Christians, with all their baggage, doctrinal deficiencies, and sometimes unchristian manners and language, will encounter as they mix with the brothers and sisters in the local church. I will go so far as to say that as a young Christian, I would have been chewed up and spit out by some of the solidly Reformed churches I am only too aware of. For twenty-nine years I was a committed Arminian in doctrine, then for years I was a half-way Calvinist, and I am yet reforming. No way would I have passed a theological examination given by some of my colleagues who hold to the doctrines of grace. And it is this that has gone wrong – grace. Grace is given by those who have had the experience of grace and know what it is that the new born, toddler, adolescent, teenager, young adult, and so on, needs from those who should be guiding, directing, and nurturing.

Therapeutic – we will always have the poor with us and whenever we can, it is our biblical responsibility to reach out, but the emphasis on the feelings and conditions of others to the exclusion of the greater need, has proved to be a distraction and diversion to the Church, whose primary mission is to proclaim the Gospel of Jesus Christ. Our needs are many and great in this often monster of a world we live in, and many are the rewards for meeting specific human needs; thus, the attraction to such is significant.

Deism – the definition here is manifold in dimension, but in the context of the CT article, I think it means a knowing about God instead of knowing God. Of course, most actual Christians worry that this may be the case with them; that is, during our spiritual struggles we suspect that we really are not born again. A mature pastor has probably run into self-identified Christians who have incredible doctrinal awareness and acuity but who display little love and devotion to the God of Scripture. This is not at all uncommon.

Now what? or So what?

This said, and assuming it approaches reality to some degree, what does it mean for me and the church of which I am pastor?

Miller Avenue Baptist Church can be a dangerous place – I have to admit this. And part of my ministry is to make our small church a safe place to grow up into the fullness of Christ. A respected friend asked me recently if I had found the churches in our county to be good homes for new born Christians to be brought up in. My answer was maybe, only maybe. I have found, unhappily, that the general Christian community can be cruel, unloving, and even brutal. But who does not know that churches can be like mine fields that are hazardous to venture into?

How can this be? First, there are moralists who look to see if people measure up. No matter how long a person has been a Christian, no matter about life circumstances, emotional maturity, and so on, some people see it as their task to watch for sin in the camp. And sin will be found, you can be sure, and too often it is broadcast about, sometimes by way of prayer requests. After four decades of pastoring, I have known and counseled many who have been needlessly scandalized by the very church families that were supposed to care for them.

Next, self-appointed theological inquisitors love to examine whether all the requisite theological, sociological, and political positions are in place. Variations or rather minor points can be dealt with somewhat severely. Thankfully, no one at the First Baptist Church of Fairfield examined my doctrinal system, which included at the time a belief in UFOs and ESP, among other strange notions. My view of the person and work of Jesus were largely lacking, and the doctrine of the Trinity – well, I did not understand anything about it. I knew two things and two things only when I was converted. One, I was a sinner, and two, Jesus was the Savior. In both of these areas, I was barely scratching the surface.

Fortunately, the doctrine of election assures us that our deficiencies in doctrine and behavior are not disqualifiers in regard to salvation. Some of us rivaled Paul for the designation, chief of sinners. But we grow up, hopefully in a loving family that knows what that is about. In the beginning it is about grace, our being rescued by a loving God in spite of ourselves through the person and work of our Lord Jesus Christ. But we – and it is a "we," since every Christian and every church is vulnerable – really do not want to end up being moralizers with proper doctrine, bent on searching out the wrong doers. Rather we want to be building each other up in love.

There is no need to wring our hands and bemoan the spiritual landscape. Let us go about our work of teaching the Bible to believers and preaching the Gospel to unbelievers, and let us not be too sure about who is who.

Twenty-Two

Christian Mystics

What is a mystic? The *Oxford Concise English Dictionary*, published by Oxford Press, has an entry: Mystic – "a person who seeks by contemplation and self-surrender to obtain unity or identity with or absorption into the Deity or the ultimate reality, or who believes in the spiritual apprehension of truths that are beyond the understanding."

On this definition we can agree. The mystic, the shaman, the santero or santera, Wiccan, medium, channeller, psychic, or yogi all rely on the "soul journey" while in an ecstasy or trance to gain such knowledge or experience. A survey of the techniques employed by various religious traditions rely on deep breathing, centering, meditation, tobacco juice, peyote, mescaline, LSD, drumming, dancing, and often these in combination, to reach the trance state. In the ecstasy or trance, entities such as animal spirits, fairies, elves, demons, angels, gods, goddesses, and others show up to guide the person on the soul journey.

But what about the **Christian** mystic? Is it normative and biblical for Christians to depend upon a trance state in order to obtain experience with his or her God? There are those in the broad Christian community who will answer yes to this question, and here I am thinking of those who practice "contemplative prayer" and hold up Theresa of Avila, St. John of the Cross, St. Ignatius of Loyola, and others, as worthy examples. For these noted Christian mystics of the past, the goal was to experience God, the very presence of God, and communicate directly with angels, saints, even Jesus.

Advocates of contemplative prayer or deep meditation suggest the following to enter into an ecstasy so that there may be an experience with Deity: Find a place alone and apart, be comfortable, calm yourself, center and ground, light a candle, breathe slowly and rhythmically, focus on the name of God or visualize Jesus, Mary, or a saint, empty the mind, focus, and open the mind and heart to whatever God will give to you.

It might be worth asking however, is this at all biblical? The answer given by some runs close to, "We may not find such instruction in the Bible, but it is not unbiblical."

Unbiblical? This is a serious question since there are so many who center on and depend upon the trance state and who are nowhere close to being either biblical or Christian. Here I have in mind the shaman, the witch, the priests and priestesses of Santería, even those who openly worship Satan. Their spiritual practices are surely to be strenuously avoided.

Some will react to the authority given the Bible; most all Christians will experience this to one degree or another at some point in their growing up. The alternative, however, is not reassuring, as cultural values come and go like the wind. Generally, we try to sanction what we want to do and what makes us feel good. But this puts us on shaky ground or even on the proverbial slippery slope. The Scripture, on the other hand, is tried in the fire and not found wanting. Great nations and peoples have been built on its foundation while those who ignore and reject the Word of God have historically not fared well. And ultimately, it is the believer's direct encounter with the Bible that is determinative.

Biblically speaking, it is clear that Satan does disguise himself as an angel of light (see 2 Corinthians 11:14-15). In addition, Jesus warned that, toward the end of history and just before the Day of Judgment, "false christs and false prophets will arise and perform great signs and wonders, so as to lead astray, if possible, even the elect" (Matthew 24:24). And perhaps the most stunning warning is Paul's: "The coming of the lawless one is by the activity of Satan with all power and false signs and wonders, and with all wicked deception for those who are perishing, because they refused to love the truth and so be saved" (2 Thessalonians 2:9-10).

How difficult it is to evaluate spiritual experiences! We tend to be accepting of these, due to their miraculous and awe-inspiring nature. Yet, the wise Christian will want to be assured that whatever spiritual practices are engaged in have both biblical ***precedent*** and ***warrant***.

The Genuine Christian Mystic

The purpose of this essay is to point out something that has been known to Christians of all varieties down through the centuries – namely, that there is indeed a Christian mysticism, one that has both biblical precedent and warrant. By ***precedent*** I mean that which is observed and practiced in Scripture. Prayer and meditation, which are mindful, alert, and conscious, are focused on God, both as to who He is and what He has done, and are clearly observed in Scripture. This is beyond dispute. Precedent: the people of God, whether seen in the New or Old Testament, prayed to and thought intensely and seriously about God.

Warrant is that which is taught in Scripture, and prayer and meditation are taught and encouraged by, among others,

David, Jesus, Paul, and John. With these then in place – precedence and warrant – prayer and meditation enjoy full biblical authority for all those in Christ who desire to seek union and deep fellowship with the Triune God.

Every person who is born from above, or born again, is indwelt by the Holy Spirit. Imagine, the Father, Son, and Holy Spirit, indwelling the believer just as He dwelt in the Holy of Holies in the Temple in Jerusalem. This Holy Spirit "bears witness with our spirit that we are children of God" (Romans 8:16). Here it is: The Holy Spirit who indwells each believer will bring to our remembrance the things that Jesus has said, as we find recorded in the New Testament (see John 14:26).

The Christian "mystic" does not therefore depend on a trance state or ecstasy to achieve experience or knowledge of God. (By the way, nowhere in Scripture is instruction to experience God and no one in Scripture set out to do so. In addition, it would also not be biblical to refer to oneself as a mystic, since such designation is not found in Scripture.) The Christian indwelt by the Spirit then has experience of God in at least two ways; one, in prayer, and two, in reading the Scripture. Both are dependent on the inner working and witness of the Holy Spirit. Neither prayer nor meditation, in their biblical context, involve an ecstasy or trance state.

In bringing our cares, requests, and words of praise and worship to God, as we are encouraged to do, we are in the very presence of God, since we are "seated" or resting with Jesus at the right hand of God the Father. Not only that, but as we study the Scripture, God reveals Himself to us as we do so. This is a most amazing experience and has meant so much to me personally as well as to millions upon millions of Christians down through the ages.

It has been my great pleasure and privilege to be a teacher and preacher of the Gospel for close to fifty years now. These responsibilities have brought me into a study of the Bible that I would probably not have known otherwise. How many dozens of times, perhaps hundreds of times, have I mentally and spiritually seen the windows of heaven opened, and in a most conscious and alert state of mind experienced God. I was not seeking such, but this would happen. I do not have the words to describe it, but the "ah-ha" moments are almost always to do with something I have learned about Jesus and His grace extended toward me. Whatever I take away from these experiences is always in harmony with mainstream and historic Christianity. Maybe I could boil it down to this: the Holy Spirit showed me more of Jesus.

Am I a Christian mystic? No, I am an ordinary follower of Jesus, probably more unspiritual than many, as I have always struggled with prayer; nonetheless, I do experience or encounter God in prayer and Bible study. And I am satisfied in my innermost being all the while living the life of a very busy, often stressed-out person in a crazy world.

Twenty-Three

Discouraged, Anyone?

Therefore, since we have been justified by faith, we have peace with God through our Lord Jesus Christ. ² Through him we have also obtained access by faith into this grace in which we stand, and we rejoice in hope of the glory of God. ³ More than that, we rejoice in our sufferings, knowing that suffering produces endurance, ⁴and endurance produces character, and character produces hope, ⁵and hope does not put us to shame, because God's love has been poured into our hearts through the Holy Spirit who has been given to us (Romans 5:1-5).

The passage is one I memorized early on in my Christian life. It has turned out to be a source of encouragement to me through many a difficult time. Since we all struggle, some more than others, my personal experience may be encouraging to someone.

The passage starts off by confirming the complete salvation we have in Christ. All our sin is forgiven, we have peace with God, and in a way we do not understand, we are in His presence, seated with Christ in the heavenly places. Jesus' work in us, that saving grace work, is finished. Now we live our lives, though they are filled with trouble and stress. We do not forget, nor minimize, what Jesus said in John 16:33: "In the world you will have tribulation. But take heart; I have overcome the world."

I will confess to you that I am vulnerable to becoming discouraged. Minor irritations and challenges, as well as big trials, like deaths in the family, being compromised by illness (we are getting older, you know), and myriads of other kinds of struggles can cause my discouragement.

Sometimes we are tempted to give up. I see this with some of the high school baseball players who quit the team because they are not as good as they thought they were, or the practices are just too hard, or they can't get along with other players, and so on. But there is another way of looking at things, another way of coping with discouraging events.

Look at the passage: sufferings produce endurance. Endurance is evidence of strength. Everybody suffers, but some are beaten down and lose strength and find themselves unreliable in the face of real life. In Christ, since we are already victorious in what really matters, we endure. We become dependable veterans in the wars of life.

Endurance then produces character. No longer defeated, needy people, we have character, are strong and courageous – not perfect, but not quitters either.

Hope then develops, personal but benefitting others as well. How we love to be around those who are survivors, who have strength of character, and who are hopeful about the future.

Real courage is not evidenced by a continual smile on the face or a false portrayal of present realities. It does not resort to hiding pain and repressing the tragic sense of life. As Christians we are not interested in fooling others to the effect that we are always chatty, bright, and upbeat. Being positive is not the same thing as biblically oriented faith; neither is it necessarily an expression of inner joy and peace.

The film roles we most admire, the heroes of the novels we read, and the stories that most inspire us are of those who endured in the face of great obstacles, who grew strong and pushed on with their lives, whether successful or not.

This is how I want to be, and I know you do too. For parents, this is what we want to show our kids. And they will learn it as it is lived out in front of them. We all have those who look to us for strength and encouragement. Hope is the ultimate fruit of learning to endure suffering,

Consider Jesus, undergoing intense suffering, enduring the cross and completing His ministry. Jesus is our great hero, our captain, and our Lord, who both embodies and imparts a hope that will not fail.

Here is how the writer of Hebrews put it:

> Therefore, since we are surrounded by so great a cloud of witnesses, let us also lay aside every weight, and sin which clings so closely, and let us run with endurance the race that is set before us, looking to Jesus, the founder and perfecter of our faith, who for the joy that was set before him endured the cross, despising the shame, and is seated at the right hand of the throne of God (Hebrews 12:1-2).

Now that is really something.

Twenty-Four

Homophobia and Heterophobia

The original title of this essay was "Homophobia and Heterophobia: Two Sides of the Same Coin?" The idea was to compare these two terms and the assumptions, perhaps fears, associated with them. Let's see how alike they really are in light of the bigger picture.

Homophobia - a hatred or fear of homosexuals (from the Oxford Concise Dictionary). This expresses the core definition of homophobia as found in most standard dictionaries.

Heterophobia - a hatred or fear of heterosexuals. This definition is not found in standard dictionaries, but the "Urban Dictionary" does not shy away from giving some rather politically incorrect definitions:

From the Urban Dictionary, found online at www.urbandictionary.com:
- Heterophobics - "Gays who are afraid of heterosexuals usually due to their own heterosexual feelings or leanings." This followed up with, "Gays, don't be afraid, you're probably just straight."
- Homophobia - "a severe condition, usually prominent in Republicans and most of American culture, leading one to: 1. inaccurately use bible quoting for the justification

of killing homosexuals; 2. restrict the rights of millions; 3. hide in their rooms crying if they looked at the male body of one of the same gender and do not vomit; 4. incessantly call things 'gay.'"
- Heterophobia - "an unreasoning disgust of heterosexuals, frequently supported by erroneous and faulty statements about heterosexuals."
- Homophobia - "the irritation of having faggotry shoved in your face."
- Heterophobics - "People who indulge in bigotry or intolerance because of the Heterophobia sickness."
- Homophobia - "an irrational fear of going home."
- Heterophobia - "The often irrational fear of heterosexuals. Usually experienced by a homosexual or bisexual who has had bad experiences with heterosexual coupling."
- Homophobia - "fear of homosexuals or possibly a condition where one person has the same fears as someone else."
- Heterophobia - "To hate heterosexuals out of some bizarre, irrational or innate fear of them. Probably due to repressed heterosexual feelings. Up with heterosexual pride!"
- Homophobia - "Dislike, fear, hatred, and/or disapproval of gays and/or homosexuality, often (but not always) for religious reasons or because of insecurity about one's sexual orientation."
- Heterophobia - "Queer frustration and hatred towards straight oppression. Often mistakenly perceived to be equivalent to homophobia, or other forms of discrimination."
- Heterophobia - "Unreasoning prejudice against heterosexuals or their sexuality, the LGBT equivalent of reverse racism, and the inverse of homophobia. Commonly manifested as disgust with the very idea of straight

sexuality and/or reproduction. It copies the prejudices of homophobia, including the idea that straightness is unnatural, or unhealthy, or can somehow be 'cured.'"
- Heterophobia - "Frequently paired with prejudice towards the opposite sex. This is surprisingly common in the LGBT community, but is often not addressed due to concerns for political correctness."

Finally, let me add this, which I gleaned and paraphrased from *Gay Religion*, edited by Scott Thumma and Edward R. Gray, and published by AltaMira Press in 2005: Some homosexuals believe homosexuality is necessary for the earth to survive, as the "breeders" keep pumping out babies, resulting in the population growing to an unsustainable level. Therefore, homosexuality is a survival mechanism.

Two sides of the same coin?

Both phobias are based on fear, or so it would seem. I would suggest that "phobia" is the wrong word to describe either phenomenon. The term means an irrational fear of something or other, such as agoraphobia - a fear of open spaces or public places. But are the so-called homo and hetero phobias based on fear? Is the homosexual fearful of heterosexuals? Is the heterosexual fearful of homosexuals?[1] In

---

1 News reports of pedophilia and of child pornography and sex slaves, both of a hetero and homo sexual nature, are frequent. For instance, in the SF Chronicle (Nov. 12, 2013) is an article entitled, "Police rescue 386 kids in global child porn bust." The arrests of 348 people, was orchestrated by Canadian police, included schoolteachers, doctors, and actors, among others. The arrests of operatives of Azov Films, that had been in business since 2005, distributed some of the most vile images of boys from age 5 to 12. "The videos included naked boys from Germany, Romania, and Ukraine which it marketed as naturist movies." This sort of thing is likely to produce some fear, and if it does not, then the human situation is more vile and evil than we have imagined.

both instances, I think not; My sense of it is that the "phobias" are something else all together.

Heterosexuals may disagree with homosexuals as to the rightness of homosexual behavior. And should they not be allowed this? Equal rights, justice, fairness, civil rights, and so on, are what most heterosexuals would agree are owed to all people regardless of sexual orientation. What if heterosexuals think homosexual behavior is "sinful" and morally wrong? Is this a bad thing?

Suppose it were a hate crime to even consider homosexual behavior wrong. Should certain kinds of thinking be criminalized? Should "homophobes "be marginalized and discriminated against? Most outrageous is the goal that anything short of complete acceptance of all that is homosexuality be stamped out and eliminated, since such thinking is the seed bed for discrimination against homosexuals. Could it be that the pro-gay, LGBT community, the whole of it or segments thereof, might even justify the creation of a "thought police" that would be dedicated to eradicating anti-homosexual thinking? Have I gone too far?

Irrational fear?

Once again let me state that to believe certain behavior is wrong is not necessarily born of fear or anxiety. There may indeed be those who are homophobic, that is, having a fear of being molested or raped by a homosexual, or fear of becoming one, or identified as being one, and the list goes on. And for those who have been in the military, or in prison, or in other circumstances where a homosexual might have a certain amount of power and authority, say a high school sports team coach, there may be homophobia, and such would not be irrational or imaginary.

Needless to say, heterosexuals in positions of power and authority over persons of the opposite sex have abused that authority in sexual ways. Certainly, there is much more of this than of homosexuals exploiting those of the same sex. Both are wrong, plain and simple.

I have been homophobic. In the Air Force there were homosexuals living in the barracks at Travis Air Force Base, and once in a while some would be caught doing what they ought not to have done and were either dishonorably discharged from the service or at least demoted and locked up for a while. In my thirty years as a volunteer at San Quentin Prison I found out that prison life was dominated by sex, some heterosexual, but mostly homosexual. I have also put five children through the school systems in Marin County, and I have been a freshman baseball coach for nine years. There are valid reasons why some have a fear of homosexuality. I don't want to get specific or graphic, but I have been there and seen that.

Yes, I have a certain amount of what is mistakenly called homophobia. So, what should be done with someone like me? Do I not have a right to it? Must the authorities be intolerant of it? As a Christian, must I repent of it?

I do not want to be fearful of homosexuals, and in fact, to the best of my ability, I am not. With the growing numbers of people coming out as gay in American, if I were homophobic I would live a fearful and miserable life. I live in the world and am very much a part of it; I am a law-abiding citizen, and I will act according to the laws of the land. But I reserve the right to believe that homosexual behavior is wrong.

For all have sinned

What about heterosexuals? Many, perhaps most, heterosexuals are disturbed sexually to one degree or another. And how would we expect anything less, particularly in western societies where sex is distorted and confused? We have rapists, child molesters, sex-slave traffickers, pimps, brothel keepers, porn addicts and makers, and more than I care to know about, and in far greater numbers than do the homosexuals. The marketplace commercializes sex and throws naked flesh before our eyes daily to sell products.

Much of the distortion has come along with the millennia-long patriarchal cultures that are in place in most parts of the world, cultures that falsely empower men to control those who are physically weaker. And our religions have either looked the other way or actually institutionalized this departure from biblical models, including Christianity. All of this morass has to do with what theologians call "the Fall," that time when humans rebelled against the Creator God (who, by the way, is both feminine and masculine, see Genesis 1:27), and sex got completely tweaked.

Moments after the Fall, Adam and Eve - or if you can't handle that, the first man and woman - looked at each other, having a new knowledge of good and evil firmly implanted in their brains, and realized they were naked and were ashamed. Wow! Ashamed and guilty - and it is right here where the trouble is. Read the account below and see what you make of it. Here is Genesis 3:1-13:

> Now the serpent was more crafty than any other beast of the field that the Lord God had made. He said to the woman, "Did God actually say, 'You shall not eat of any tree in the garden'?" [2] And the woman said to the serpent, "We may eat of the fruit of the trees in the garden, [3] but God said, 'You shall not eat of the fruit of the tree that is in the midst of the garden, neither shall you touch it, lest you die.'" [4] But the serpent said to the woman, "You will not surely die. [5] For God knows that when you eat of it your eyes will be opened, and you will be like God, knowing good and evil." [6] So when the woman saw that the tree was good

for food, and that it was a delight to the eyes, and that the tree was to be desired to make one wise, she took of its fruit and ate, and she also gave some to her husband who was with her, and he ate. ⁷ Then the eyes of both were opened, and they knew that they were naked. And they sewed fig leaves together and made themselves loincloths. ⁸ And they heard the sound of the Lord God walking in the garden in the cool of the day, and the man and his wife hid themselves from the presence of the Lord God among the trees of the garden. ⁹ But the Lord God called to the man and said to him, "Where are you?" ¹⁰ And he said, "I heard the sound of you in the garden, and I was afraid, because I was naked, and I hid myself." ¹¹ He said, "Who told you that you were naked? Have you eaten of the tree of which I commanded you not to eat?" ¹² The man said, "The woman whom you gave to be with me, she gave me fruit of the tree, and I ate." ¹³ Then the Lord God said to the woman, "What is this that you have done?" The woman said, "The serpent deceived me, and I ate."

Guilt and Shame

A careful interpreter could reel off pages of commentary and never get to the bottom of all that is in the above passage. But there is certainly guilt and shame.

The balance between the man and the woman was gone. Together they reflected the Creator; now separate and apart life drastically changed and not for the better. Heterosexual marriage is now a mere shadow of what it was intended to be. Not until that which is called heaven and paradise, symbolized as a wedding between Christ, the groom, and the Church, His bride, will there be restitution and realization of the original intent of the Creator. Until then, well, we know the story, don't we?

Pleasure, contentment, fulfillment, completion, happiness, rightness - it was all there for Adam and Eve. These wonderful gifts were replaced with guilt and an abiding sense of shame. No matter how much pleasure might be found in a sexual act, it would never be, for anyone, what it could have been. So we have sin lodged right in the core of the identity of the human sexual experience. And heteros and homos have forever attempted to overcome guilt and shame.

Within marriage between a man and a woman, however flawed and imperfect, is contained a hint and a promise of what will come in the grand *eschaton*, that end point when there will be a recreation and a new heaven and a new earth. What God started will be completed. God's laws, the thou-shalt-nots, were intended to make the best of what is. Adultery, fornication, and homosexual acts are a breaking of the law, and thus guilt and shame arise. That is just how it is.

Though the LGBT community may succeed in all its demands for equality and normality, guilt and shame will remain. Could it be that the homosexual, who in the quest to eradicate homophobia, is really being driven by guilt and shame? If homosexual behavior is normal and good, then ought not the negative and powerful emotions go away? But they will not go away, since the 'wrongness experience' is hard wired into every human being.

God made sex and meant it for both procreation and pleasure; it is a strong bond that keeps a husband and wife together. It is in that "one flesh" relationship where sex can be experienced absent guilt and shame. God-ordained and -approved sex is a wonderful thing. A marriage between a man and a woman allows for the freedom to develop a very sexy relationship, which is not driven by lust and a never-ending quest for fulfillment. Such a sexuality opens a door to a "peaceful easy feeling."

Is achieving equality enough?

Victory won, normalcy and equality achieved, backed by the law of the land, and clear sailing ahead. All will be well, right? This has certainly not been so for heterosexuals, and the trend seems to be downward rather than the other way around. Will homosexuals fare better? Probably not.

Sexuality is the human core identity, but it is not larger than the kingdom of God and life eternal. The fuss about homo and hetero phobias is magnified, because sex has become so very distorted and filled up with the hope of ultimate satisfaction. In sexuality, even for the most well adjusted and blissful heterosexual married couple, there will be disappointment and frustration. As they say, "Get over it."

Phobias must not drive our behavior

Both hetero and homo phobias are expressions of sinfulness, not the sense of fear itself, but the acting out on the fears to the detriment of others. We are called to love our neighbor as ourselves, so we have to admit that expressing these phobias is wrong. At least, let us deal humanely and rationally with each other, homosexual and heterosexual. Let us hear and respect each other's positions while not having to approve of them.

If I could say that homosexual behavior is right, I would do so, but I cannot. I cannot say that the heterosexual's adulteries and fornications are right, either. To approve homosexuality in any form, or to approve sex outside of marriage, is unacceptable from a biblical perspective. And to many, such is unacceptable.

There is hope, strength, and dignity in saying "No." The aberrational, criminal, abusive, or exploitive quest for self-centered sexual pleasure cannot be tolerated by a civilized society where the rights of the weak must be safeguarded. Watching someone head off the steep cliff without shouting out a warning is both negligence and unloving to the extreme.

Enough of this phobia talk.

Twenty-Five

Mindfulness: Another View

In the Sunday *Washington Post* of May 25, 2014, is a story about a Buddhist teacher/therapist who works with military veterans suffering from Post Traumatic Stress Disorder. As outlined by the Post journalist, her theory of "mindfulness" contends that keeping one's mind on the here and now is healing.

Her approach seems to recommend focusing on oneself, centering on where one is and how one feels right now. Question: Is this ego-centric? If you think about others or the troubles you are presently facing, are you not being mindful?

Perhaps being mindful is beneficial, but like everything else, that is debatable. I suspect some will find a measure of relief while others will not.

Mindfulness! I read and hear of this often, since I live in Mill Valley, California, a bastion for Buddhist and yoga-style meditators. One of my friends at our local gym is the director of a Zen center, and he and I have talked on and off over the years on the subject of mindfulness.

Mindfulness! I suppose one ought to be mindful. It sounds like a good thing, maybe even a virtue. Mindful *of* the moment, mindful *in* the moment; it seems like a worthy goal,

I suppose. Certainly, if a train were bearing down on you, you would want to be mindful of yourself, exactly where you were at in that moment.

To ask, mindful of what, probably misses the point. I don't think it is about jumping out of the way of trains, planes, or automobiles, but it might encompass such. It seems like a koan, one of those sayings that leave a person scratching his or her head, like "What is the sound of one hand clapping?"

This is now bordering on being silly; even I know it. I am not mindless. Let me get down to it: I am suspicious that what the mindfulness practitioner means is she has discovered something very large, and that those who do not practice mindfulness are missing out.

I also wonder if the call to mindfulness is not a form of Buddhist evangelism. There is a Christian type of evangelism that basically looks like a presentation of their gospel, using a three-part formula: Law plus Grace = Gospel. The Christian evangelist points out that the Law of Moses, whose centerpiece is the Ten Commandments of Exodus chapter 20, will lead the reader to understand that they have sinned and fallen well short of God's demands. Bad News. The second part of the formula is Grace, which means that, although God could send the poor Law breaker to hell, He instead pardons, forgives, and saves the miserable sinner. Good News. The result is Gospel, which literally means Good News. Shocking! Instead of hell there is now heaven.

So then, is there anything of a mindful nature here? It is self-focused to a considerable degree, and it centers on really large issues that impact the here and now. It is ultimate present conversation between the Creator and creature. How much more significant, even mindful, can you get?

Mindfulness. The impression I often get is that the Buddhist, or perhaps the Hindu yogi – those who meditate and focus on the NOW – are where one *ought* to be as opposed to those Christian types who are thinking only about the kingdom to come with the harps, angel wings, and fluffy clouds in the sweet bye and bye, which is down the road someplace and certainly not in the here and now. The Buddhist version of the good news is put forth as superior to the Christian version. Of course, like everything else, this is debatable.

I am mindful that living in the now is a good thing. I embrace that concept, but is that all there is? Since there is a future, however short or long, there is more to life than now. And now is not that exciting or even pleasant. Sometimes now is painful, discouraging, and boring, and I would rather not focus on it.

However, rather than stepping out of the suffering of now by eliminating a sense of time at all, I prefer hope. Hope is a good thing; hope is future-oriented and centers on what one desires to happen. The Christian's hope, however, is not wishful thinking, but sure. Another word for it is "faith," a God-given "assurance of things hoped for, the conviction of things not seen" (Hebrews 11:1).

"My hope is built on nothing less than Jesus' blood and righteousness." This opening line from a wonderful hymn entitled "The Solid Rock" states it clearly and succinctly. My mind is focused on what the God of creation has done that I could never do: remove my sin and make me his own, for all the now left in eternity.

I prefer this state of mindfulness.

Twenty-Six

Got an App?

When the newly drafted football player, Michael Sam, kissed his "wife" (boyfriend), someone was unthinking enough to express disapproval, actually disgust, and the gay activists attacked. A guy named Ward expressed less than positive feelings about seeing this scene on TV and began receiving death threats; his kids were included in the murderous threats, too.

Didn't Ward deserve what he got? After all, the guy dared to have thoughts about seeing one man kissing another on television. But Ward didn't *do* anything – didn't deny anyone their equal rights or cause anything to happen for which he could even be sued. What he did was to think and express something that offended and provoked the Gay Gestapo thought police.

The media, out of the usual fear of being attacked by the Gay Gestapo, never uttered a word in defense of Ward, not even regarding the death threats against him or his family. Yes, here was a vile homophobe who deserved to be punished.

Homophobic. Is that a fear of homosexuals? Is it a fear of being homosexual? Fear is an emotion and is mostly involuntary. Thinking or feeling that homosexual behavior is immoral is probably common for the majority of Americans, and this is not overt and intended discrimination against homosexuals, which is a violation of a person's civil rights, and which is wrong. But does not wanting to be homosexual or experiencing disgust when seeing gay behavior on mainstream media constitute homophobia? No, discomfort with, disapproval of, or even disgust at, immoral and unnatural behavior are not fear-based reactions.

But they are reactions, and reactions are generated in the brain, and even subtle brain waves can be detected by monitors running electronic applications. Do you suppose an app will be developed that will detect anti-gay thoughts going through the brain? And if so, who will receive the data and what will be the punishment?

The pro-gay lobby has successfully punished and shut down nearly all descent. If a retailer does or sells something that offends them, they start a boycott, and vendors who wholesale products to the store will be attacked as well. If a public figure utters even a slightly anti-gay statement, he or she must grovel before the media inquisitors, who are no more than surrogates for the gay lobby, hoping to regain a good name.

I wonder if we are not seeing a kind of revenge from the gay population for the mistreatment they have experienced over the years. Despite their inevitable guilt and shame, they want to be seen as normal and accepted like everyone else, but they've been seen as less than okay by others, even considered to be sinners by Christians like me, and that may have become intolerable for some. So, like begets like?

How long will knee-jerk reactions from gays on the emotional edge advance their cause? Will the pendulum swing back into a kind of balance?

Yes, that is possible, I think. But things will never be the same as in previous generations, say in the 1950s. We are looking at a new normal, in which the norm is tinged with a kind of perverseness – sorry, but that's what I am thinking and feeling. I will never accept this new "business as usual" that our society has been cowed into accepting. Hope you can get over it, since I and hosts like me are not likely to change, despite the threats, boycotts, mudslinging, civil suits, and bad publicity.

Apple, Samsung, Microsoft, or Google – which will be the first to come up with the app?

Twenty-Seven

God's Will is Simple and Clear

About two years after my new birth I became obsessed with wanting to know what God's will was for me. I heard appeals from the pulpit to surrender to foreign missions or to answer the call to full time pastoral ministry. The trouble was, though I wanted both and was ready to do either, I could not be sure if I was called to either.

The tension I experienced coalesced one day while studying for a master's degree in psychology. It suddenly dawned on me that I would not be able to talk to counselees about Jesus in a school setting as a student counselor. Then my emotional and spiritual difficulty dissolved as I made a decision to attend seminary with a view to being a pastor. I did have a sense of being called, like Isaiah the prophet or even like Paul, so I announced to my pastor that I had received a call, and, realizing that a new semester was about to start, hurriedly went off to attend classes at Golden Gate Baptist Theological Seminary in Marin County, CA.

This essay is not, however, about experiencing a call. To this day I believe my calling was genuinely from God. This essay is about knowing what the will of God is. My objective is to be as biblical as possible, though the answer might seem rather tame and plain.

In former days

Countless times while a hippie street Christian in San Francisco's Haight-Ashbury District in the 1960s, I used *The Four Spiritual Laws* booklet published by Campus Crusade for Christ. It correctly stated that God does have a plan for the Christian's life. The question was, how do I find out what that plan is?

Thus ensued numbers of mechanisms, everything from filling out questionnaires to having "prophets" pray that they might get a "word from God." As I pastored a church filled with young adults in the 1970s, many of whom were avidly seeking to serve their Lord, we of the pastoral staff and elders sought diligently to find answers and help people discover God's will for their lives. While we were at it, we also tried to discover their spiritual gifts. Looking back, I think that what we really did was process, almost unconsciously, what we knew about a person and consider what they were already doing in their lives thus far, in order to come up with something that seemed reasonable. The trouble was that our pronouncements were usually preceded by a "Thus saith the Lord. . ." Few had the maturity to challenge these supposed words from God.

God's will is the same for us all

We really just needed to trust Scripture and make it clear and simple: God's will is that we believe in his Son, Jesus. To a group of seekers who asked Jesus, "What must we do, to be doing the works of God?" [1] (John 6:28), Jesus answered in verse 29, "This is the work of God, that you believe in him

---

[1] Works and will are essentially synonymous, as can be deduced, since in Jesus' response to the question He uses the term "will" in place of "works." See John 6:39-40.

whom he has sent." Overshadowing all else, the chief will of God for us is to believe in, rely upon, or trust in the Triune God for the forgiveness of sin and our new birth. Jesus is extremely clear: "For this is the will of my Father, that everyone who looks on the Son and believes in him should have eternal life, and I will raise him up on the last day" (John 6:40).

We start our Christian lives by trusting in Jesus, and we continue the same way. It is as the writer of Hebrews states:

> Therefore, since we are surrounded by so great a cloud of witnesses, let us also lay aside every weight, and sin which clings so closely, and let us run with endurance the race that is set before us, looking to Jesus, the founder and perfecter of our faith, who for the joy that was set before him endured the cross, despising the shame, and is seated at the right hand of the throne of God (Hebrews 12:1-2).

God's will is that we grow up in Christ, continually turning away from sin, and should we falter, confess our sins and receive his forgiveness (see 1 John 1:8-2:2). We are to be perfect, or complete and mature followers of Jesus, and we know this does not happen overnight.

We take on the full armor of God that we may be strong in the Lord and stand against the wiles of the devil (see Ephesians 6:10-20).

We are to flee from sin, study and meditate on Scripture, pray and in the way Jesus taught us (see Matthew 6:9-13), and a whole host of other instructions found bunched together in the Sermon on the Mount in Matthew chapters 5, 6, and 7, but also found scattered throughout the whole of Scripture, Genesis to Revelation.

Every Christian is to be a proclaimer of the Good News

that in Jesus' work on the cross we can be forgiven and receive the gift of eternal life. Here is what Jesus specifically said:

> All authority in heaven and on earth has been given to me. Go therefore and make disciples of all nations, baptizing them in the name of the Father and of the Son and of the Holy Spirit, teaching them to observe all that I have commanded you (Matthew 28:18-20).

Details are simply that: details

The "when," "where," "what," and "how" are just details. These details, however, adopt a place that is most often exaggerated, that is at minimum of secondary importance. Wherever I am, I am a follower of Jesus and live to bring Him glory and honor. However I go about this is of less significance than that I go ahead and be a witness. *When* and *where* are when and where it is possible. The *why* is what is important: that to serve Him and be a witness is enough. This last "detail" remains consistently true, whereas the when, where, what, and how will change from time to time.

The will of God is not a mystery to be solved; we already have in Scripture enough information. The will of God is not a secret to be discovered. The revelation of the will of God is plain for all Bible lovers to see.

Twenty-Eight

Something Good about Hell

Why all the fuss about hell? Hell is probably not as bad as it seems. Hell is also the preferred destination for most. Up until a certain time in my twenty-first year of life I would not have wanted to go to heaven and be with all those holy types.

Hell, however, is not a silly superstition. In fact, there is a perfectly good reason for it.

What or When or Where is Hell?

There was a time when there was no hell. Jesus pointed this out in Matthew 25:41: "Then he will say to those on his left, 'Depart from me, you cursed, into the eternal fire prepared for the devil and his angels.'" Those "on his left" ignored and rejected Jesus as the Messiah and Savior, but my focus is on the word "prepared." There had to be a place where the devil and his angels, the unclean spirits or demons, must dwell forever.[1]

---

1 Hell may have existed prior to the creation of the universe. This all depends on the initial rebellion of Lucifer. It is a controversial subject, some holding that the demonic rebellion occurred before the creation itself and some contending afterward. Which is which lies in the mystery of God, but that hell exists now and is eternal is a settled biblical doctrine.

Notice however, there will *not* be a time when hell is *not* – it is *now* eternal.

Hell is described as "outer darkness" (See Matthew 8:12, 22:13, and 25:30, a Jewish idiom essentially meaning a place of aloneness without light or any good thing.

Hell is also described as a place of "weeping and gnashing of teeth," which is another common Jewish idiom and was doubtless well known to Jesus and His hearers. The phrase describes something utterly horrid: a mindful, emotional terror unbounded (See Matthew 8:12, 13:42, 22:13, 24:51, 25:30; and Luke 13:28.

So then, what is so good about hell?

Hell is the preferred destination for many; heaven is the preferred destination for a few. This we know from what Jesus said, as found in Matthew 7:13:

> "Enter by the narrow gate. For the gate is wide and the way is easy that leads to destruction, and those who enter by it are many. For the gate is narrow and the way is hard that leads to life, and those who find it are few."

It is only obvious: heaven is for those who are eagerly looking forward to being in His presence, and hell is for those who despise such an eternity. In this way, hell is more than fair and gracious treatment.

Why should this be?

Hell is an existence where all ungodliness is banished right along with the devil and his angels. But, and this is a huge BUT, sin will be there in its entire twisted perverseness. In stark contrast, there will be no evil in heaven, since it cannot and will not be in His presence.

God is completely holy, and anyone not made holy, who thus hates and dreads holiness, would absolutely not want to be in the presence of God. Consider even Adam and Eve, who hid from God's presence after they sinned, whereas, before that, they had wonderful communion with him (see Genesis 3:1-13).

A personal note

Prior to my conversion, I did not like even being around Christians. I could barely tolerate them. In a way I cannot explain, I preferred my good old buddies to the few Christians I knew. These latter made me feel bad, made me feel I was being judged by them, though there was nothing said to indicate it. In college, I had to write a philosophy paper that necessitated my attending several churches. Just sitting through a Sunday morning service gave me fairly high anxiety. This all changed upon my new birth and the opposite happened. From then on I enjoyed, even loved, being with other Christians.

What is so bad about heaven?

We commonly see cartoons depicting holy types in white robes with halos, playing harps and sitting on clouds in heaven doing little and even complaining about their lot. And we laugh at these caricatures. It conveys to the popular culture distorted ideas about heaven. However, heaven is the deepest desire of the human heart and mind. Being in communion with the Creator, being at perfect peace, with joy abounding, where love is supreme and everlasting, not to mention the complete absence of death, disease, sin, devil or demons, and much more than words can convey - this is real paradise.

Heaven, the only "place" where God dwells, is the fulfillment and realization of all that is possible. But this only for those who love their God and Savior. Otherwise, heaven would seem awful and fearful. To stand clothed or covered in guilt and shame forever before the One who righteously judges sin would be more than anyone could bear.

It is either fear or love

Following their law breaking Adam and Eve hid from God, which is only natural. We hide from God as well, because we are law-breakers and fear His presence. Somewhere hard-wired into us is a fear of judgment, a fear of standing naked before a holy and righteous Judge who knows everything about us. We stand condemned without defense. Though we might laugh at such a thought, it will not go away quietly. There is something awful about heaven and good about hell.

No one will love being in hell. There the power of evil is unrestrained, with no shield from the most horrible of abuses.

Christians love the name of Jesus; we love what He has done for us. We delight in singing His praises and expressing our love for our God and Savior -- something we never tire of in spite of occasional droughts and discouragements. And in heaven, in His presence forever, the forever will be one of unbounded and unrestrained love. What a difference!

Twenty-Nine

The Anointing. The Anointing. The Anointing.

"The Anointing – this is the whole thing, isn't it?"

That is what I heard Paul Cain say some ten years ago at a nearby Pentecostal church.

Reverend Cain is a big name among the so-called Kansas City Prophets, along with a number of others like Bob Jones, Mike Bickel, Rick Joiner, John Paul Jackson, Francis Frangipane, Lou Engle, and James Goll. The Apostolic-Prophetic Movement,[1] sometimes known as the Third Wave, was to be the re-establishment of the Five-Fold ministry of apostle, prophet, evangelist, pastor and teacher as found in Ephesians 4.[2] These leaders saw themselves as part of the

---

1   C. Peter Wagner is often recognized as an "apostle" in the recreation of the "Five Fold Ministry," and by virtue of his position as a professor at Fuller Theological Seminary in Pasadena, California, and his part in launching the Church Growth seminars at Fuller (of which I was a part), he provided prestige and clout to the fledgling "Third Wave" revival.

2   Rather than five ministries of apostle, prophet, evangelist, pastor, and teacher, many combine pastor and teacher, since the two are joined by the Greek co-coordinating conjunction kai or "and." More correctly, it is the four-fold ministry. And it may be noted that, while these ministries or offices may not always have been formally established, they have never be absent in the long history of the Church.

reconstitution of the fabled biblical model meant to operate in the "last days." And for such a grand vision, a special and super powerful anointing would be required.

Rodney M. Howard-Browne

I was wondering, then, if the anointing Cain talked about was the same that Rodney M. Howard-Browne purportedly brought to America from his home in South Africa. It was Howard-Browned who strongly influenced the "revival" that came to the Toronto Airport Vineyard Church in Canada. It was there that Randy Clark received the anointing from Howard-Browne and spread the "fire" of the revival.

Howard-Browne, in his books *Flowing in the Holy Ghost* (FHG) and *Flowing in the Holy Spirit* (FHS), describes that anointing.[3] It is essential and necessary to define what Howard-Browne means by anointing as presented in the two books mentioned above.

In FHG he says, "the anointing is the presence of God. . . that will come and begin to touch people" (p. 13). "I wait for the unction all the time; I wait for the burning of the Spirit of God within. That burning, that churning, bubbles like a boiling pot inside, because that's what the word 'prophesy' means" (p. 14).

Howard-Browne says, "you must stir yourself up for the gifts to begin to operate" (p. 14). Therefore, after stirring, "it will happen automatically. God will begin to move" (p. 15).

In a section labeled "When the Anointing Falls" he says, "I began to speak supernaturally. I became another person!. . . It's almost like I'm standing outside my body, hearing myself prophesy. . .People begin to shake and fall out under the power of God in their seats as the word of the Lord comes forth. No one touches them" (p. 31). He goes on: "You can't

---

3 The two books are virtually identical in content, having only minor variations and additions. To read one is to read the other.

say, 'I'm going to get up and prophesy now.' However, you can prepare for the anointing to prophesy. You do this by stirring yourself up, by preparing your heart, and by waiting on the Spirit of God. Then, when the anointing comes, you flow with it. But you can only prophesy when the anointing comes!'" (p. 31).

Randy Clark

Not everyone got the anointing, not even those who actually touched Browne. Randy Clark, who had reportedly gotten the anointing, was also able to pass it on to others, or so it was claimed. He also met with those in Toronto, and people touched him – some got it, but most did not.

A contingent from our local ministerial association visited Toronto, and after they returned we gathered in a meeting. There we were, expecting something big. But even for those who got close to the "anointed" people and even touched one of them, nothing happened. Though disappointed, we planned another trip.

I saw Randy Clark personally some years ago in Redding, California, when he visited the Bethel Church pastored by Bill Johnson, whom I guessed had gotten the anointing. The anointing was power, and power was what it was all about – the power to heal and do miracles. Many of those present had miracle stories: crowns of gold on teeth; gold dust in their hair; feathers mysteriously floating down from the ceiling; people raised from the dead (none were confirmed); people healed from stomach and back pain or from chronic migraines; youth healed instantaneously from addictions to pot and pills. Oddly, the two members of Bethel who brought me there, both with some serious bodily ailments, were never themselves healed, nor did they know anyone personally who had actually been healed. The miracle stories circulated around town, surfacing occasionally, but somehow those who were healed could not be located. This was no doubt a miracle, too.

Do I sound irreverent or judgmental? Am I being a God mocker and thus in danger of committing blasphemy against the Holy Spirit?[4] Could I be standing against the flowing of the river of the Spirit now moving in these last days? Am I foolishly, even rebelliously, refusing to ride the wave? Frankly, these kinds of mind-think, conformist charges are enough to shame and shut-up most questioners, but not everyone is falling in line or is so lacking in confidence in the saving grace of Jesus that they stop thinking and evaluating.

Cain's anointing

Paul Cain rambled on for an hour and finally starting indicating that he was about to reveal the biggie, the real deal, the ultimate, that one great thing that meant absolutely everything. Wow, the anticipation was palpable. Cain moved toward the front of the stage. He stood stone still. He stretched out his left arm, his brown eyes scanning the congregation, now speechless, motionless, while we waited without a sound. And then it came, what we were all waiting for: "The Anointing. The Anointing. The Anointing." He said it was the anointing.

To demonstrate the anointing he stared at a number of the faithful sitting in the front row.[5] One by one he told their fortunes. He said he saw a television set-like thing over each one's head and could watch their futures unfold before his

---

4 *The God Mockers* is the title of a book written by Stephen Hill who was the principle evangelist for the Brownsville Revival in Pensacola, Florida during the mid-1990s. All those who rejected the idea that it was a genuine outpouring of the Holy Spirit he so labeled.

5 I had gotten in place early and was a little surprised at how ushers brought in, paraded might be a better word, a group of people and seated them directly in front of the platform. The reason for this became clear later on.

very eyes. One would be a great prophet in Africa. Another would be greatly used of God in Asia as a healer. One young lady would found a school for orphans in South America. Without exception, each person would do something wonderful in the kingdom of God. Cain could see it on the television screens. It was the anointing that made it all happen.

Kundalini and Shaktipat

Over the years I've talked with a number of so-called prophets and healers who spoke like Howard-Browne. A burning power rising up in their bodies that gave them power to do miracles. During my days in the Jesus People Movement, when we did see miracles, I never experienced or heard about anything like what Howard-Browne described. However, I have had and continue to have conversations with those involved in various spiritual practices that do sound like what Howard-Browne described. I turned to Wikipedia for the material I suspected I would find:

> **Kundalini** is described within eastern religious or spiritual traditions as "an indwelling spiritual energy that can be awakened in order to purify the subtle system and ultimately to bestow the state of Yoga, or Divine Union, upon the 'seeker' of truth." "The Yoga Upanishads describe Kundalini as lying 'coiled' at the base of the spine, represented as either a goddess or sleeping serpent waiting to be awakened." In physical terms, one commonly reported Kundalini experience is a feeling like electric current running along the spine.
>
> **Kundalini** can be awakened by shaktipat – spiritual transmission by a Guru or teacher – or by spiritual practices such as yoga or meditation. Sometimes

Kundalini reportedly awakens spontaneously as the result of physical or psychological trauma, or even for no apparent reason.

One man said he felt an activity at the base of his spine starting to flow, so he relaxed and allowed it to happen. A feeling of surging energy began traveling up his back, and at each chakra he felt an orgasmic electric feeling like every nerve trunk on his spine beginning to fire. A second man described a similar experience but accompanied by a wave of euphoria and happiness softly permeating his being. He described the surging energy as being like electricity traveling from the base of his spine to the top of his head. He said the more he analyzed the experience, the less it occurred.

Kundalini can also awaken spontaneously, for no obvious reason, or be triggered by intense personal experiences such as accidents, near death experiences, childbirth, emotional trauma, extreme mental stress, and so on. Some sources attribute spontaneous awakenings to the "grace of God," or possibly to spiritual practice in past lives.

The popularization of eastern spiritual practices has been associated with psychological problems in the West. Psychiatric literature notes that "since the influx of eastern spiritual practices and the rising popularity of meditation starting in the 1960s, many people have experienced a variety of psychological difficulties, either while engaged in intensive spiritual practice or 'spontaneously'.

I could go on, but I think the above is enough. However,

one last observation might be of value. On the fourth page of the Wikipedia article on Kundalini is a section with the heading, "Physical and psychological effects." In brief, I list some of the items which are referred to as the "Kundalini syndrome:"

> involuntary jerks, tremors, shaking, itching, tingling, and crawling sensations; energy rushes or feelings of electricity circulating the body; intense heat (heating) or cold; trance-like and altered states of consciousness; disrupted sleep pattern; loss of appetite or overeating; mood swings with periods of depression or mania.

The quest for power
Certainly Howard-Browne and any of the Kansas City Prophets and those associated with Rick Joyner of Morningstar in North Carolina, Mike Bickle of IHOP in Kansas City, Bill Johnson at Bethel Church in Redding, California, or anyone else associated with the Third Wave would not knowingly embrace anything to do with Kundalini or shaktipat, but there is an obvious association if not direct connection. That association could well be the quest for power.

Power, the one great and overriding drive behind the occult, is the great lure. So much of the tragedy of humanity has been the direct result of striving to acquire and retain power. The quest for magical powers to heal drives shamanism and religions like Santería. The neo-pagan religions like Wicca also focus on power to heal and perform magic. How thin the line can be that separates the occult and pagan from the biblically orthodox.

Anyone who has either read of or experienced firsthand a great moving of the Holy Spirit desires to see it happen again. In our impatience and longing for the excitement of such times, we attempt to "work up" such a revival or awakening ourselves. We can go to extremes and "work up" the crowd with music and great expectations of miracles and pass them off as a genuine move of the Holy Spirit. In my view, the epitome of error is the concept of deliberately obtaining an anointing, which is a special and rare gift of the Holy Spirit and not ours for the grabbing. One way of identifying authentic Christianity is that Jesus Christ and Him crucified is front and center.

Off the charts

But then I think: no, wait a minute. These guys up in Redding at Bethel and in Kansas City say we are "off the charts." Their prophets declare that these are the last days, and the Bible is not so important anymore. After all, many are conversing with angels now, even big name angels, and some are speaking directly with Jesus as one would in a phone call.[6] People like Kat Kerr are going directly to God, bypassing angels altogether. Yes, she reports face to face meetings with the Creator of heaven and earth in the "throne room" where she gets the real scoop about the last of the last days. Apparently, we are right up there at a few seconds before midnight on the great cosmic clock. Wow, I'm a believer!

Going corporate?

Am I making fun? Yes I am to a degree, in order to highlight the ridiculousness of the whole thing. And one wonders, what comes next? I mean, where can you go next? After hearing from God personally and getting the definitive word about the wrap-up of history from the Big Guy, everything else seems second rate, not to mention a waste of time.

---

6 This is what Sarah Young does as she journals in her books like Jesus Calling.

Someone who has followed the whole enterprise in Redding surmised that they have shifted into "corporate" mode to fill a possible void, by which he meant the peddling of products – everything from books, videos, and worship music, which one would expect, to dietary supplements, clothing, exercise plans and equipment, and whatever else these entrepreneurs think will sell. God help us.

Could the newly and self-ordained apostles and prophets walk away from all of this, with the requirement to denounce it? Think of the humiliation, embarrassment, sinking salaries, dried up speaking engagements, rejections, tongue-wagging, falling book sales, mounting property payments, and the disappearing praise of the crowds? What would they do – retire, repent, step down, and confess, with their lives and ministries exposed as a fraud? What do they do after making shipwreck of their faith and the faith of many thousands of others? Here is where the miracles are needed.

Closing comment

I am one who has made major errors in my life and ministry, and from these I am yet greatly pained and will be until I get home. Indeed, the sufferings of this present time, whether the result of the Fall or my own rebellious folly, are not worth comparing with what God has prepared for us. My repenting will last my whole life, and though I may be embarrassed in certain circles, yet I take confidence that all my sin has been atoned for through the shedding of the precious blood of the Lamb. Thus it is with confidence that I continue following Jesus and rejoicing in the ability to yet be a servant in His kingdom. The audience, after all, is not in the pews but in heaven.

Thirty

The Contract

During the four decades plus that I have been a pastor, I have not owned a home. For twenty-six years, it was my pleasure to live rent free in a parsonage. But always prior to that I paid rent.

Renting is a collateral contract. That is, both parties have to perform. I have to pay rent in a timely manner, and in return, the landlord must allow me to live in his house. If I cannot pay, then out I go – evicted. During tight times (and there have been plenty of those) it was somewhat scary to think of being tossed out, family and all.

One-Party Contract

A unilateral contract, on the other hand, is one where only one party in the agreement must perform. It is not equal; one party controls the entire contract. There is a scary nature to this sort of arrangement, because one party is at the mercy of the other. And given the peculiar nature of people, one is never secure in the knowledge that the agreement will hold firm.

You may see where I am going, but let me draw it out a bit more.

The contract I have with my Savior and Lord is a unilateral one, in which he is the performing party. It must be this way, because I could not perform under the terms of a bilateral contract. Why not? Because the contract demands sinless perfection, and I cannot uphold my side of that requirement.

One little breach of a collateral contract, whether minor or major, would be enough to nullify the entire agreement and subject me to penalties. However I might try to meet the requirements, I would at some point fail. Frankly, I do fail inevitably, quickly, and regularly.

However, here is the good news. My Lord Jesus performs constantly, did perform completely, and will perform forever. He satisfies the contract on my behalf. Therefore, I have no fear of failure at all.

This faithfulness on my Savior's part inspires me to please him and honor him. When I consider how unworthy I am and how worthy he is, the amazing nature of it all sometimes overwhelms me.

Greatly Mistaken

How desperate it would be if I had to perform – either to enter into the contract in the first place or to keep it alive. Indeed, how hopeless is any form of collateral contract with God, where the downside is eternal separation from him in hell. Yet, this is exactly the kind of contract that so many believe in and desire.

They are told that God's performance in Christ is good and powerful, but something more is required of them to fulfill the contract. They are told they *can* fulfill it, *should* fulfill it, and must fulfill it, since if they fail to do so at any point they stand in danger of losing everything.

But those who believe such things are greatly mistaken. The gospel is unilateral in nature. It must be, because none of us are able to meet the requirements of a righteous God. We have broken God's holy ordinances repeatedly, because we have a fallen nature which propels us into law breaking.

God Acts Alone

As a believer in Jesus Christ, and one born of the Spirit, I have the Spirit of Christ within me, helping my infirmities. That means that I can yield the "fruit of the Spirit" which pleases God – love, joy, peace, patience, and so much else (Galatians 5:22-23). But the point is that I also retain my old sinful nature, so that I cannot obey God with the perfection and consistency that he requires to justify and accept me in my own right.

That is why God must act alone to meet the requirements of the contract. He imputes to me Christ's *perfect* righteousness, removes the penalties of my violations, and gifts me with eternal life.

And *this* contract, controlled completely by God, is not scary – because I know I am loved by him. Its very purpose is that I might be "holy and without blame before him in love" (Ephesians 1:4). He will never reject me despite my repeated, though regrettable, failures.

I refuse to sign any bilateral contract with God and will make no effort to ask others to do so either.

Thirty-One

Adam and Eve in the History of Salvation

Other titles for this essay could be:

- "Origins: What Are We to Make of It in Light of the Bible and Evolutionary Science?"
- "A Theological Conversation: What to Do with Adam and Evolution?"
- "Is Scripture Right About Adam? If So, Is It Wrong about Evolution? How Might a Biblically Faithful Christian Make Sense of It All?

Let us explore the issue, and maybe we can figure out which title is the most accurate.

Positions Christians take

There are three general positions regarding the relationship of biblical origins to contemporary evolutionary science held among Christians: creationism, intelligent design, and theistic evolution.[1] Not always obvious is the fact that this

---

1 The following descriptions are radically condensed and simplified, and this essay is merely an opening statement which looks forward to more conversation and debate.

conversation or debate is actually an intra-mural rather than an extra-mural one. By that I mean, it is a conversation or debate that goes on among Christians who all want to be biblically faithful, so that it ought to be conducted in a civil and brotherly manner.

Creationism may primarily accept either a very young earth creation date or a little older young earth creation date. With the former the year 4004 B.C. is pegged as the year of creation while the latter holds to dates of around 10,000 B.C. Both subscribe to the earth being created old-appearing; however, some of the mainline young earth creationists insist that the flood of Noah's era was all that was necessary for the earth to have attained its present oldish appearance.

A creationist also believes that the entire universe was created by a supernatural being, and for Christians, this being is God as described in the Bible. In the generic sense, all Christians, whether young earth or oldish earth creationists, intelligent design advocates, or theistic evolutionists are all creationists; it is simply the how of it all which is at issue.

After science developed concepts about origins in the 18th century onwards, efforts were made by Christians to reconcile the new views with the Bible and its Genesis accounts of creation. By the beginning of the 20th century the creation-evolution controversy had developed, largely fomented by the popularity of Charles Darwin's work, and the term "creationist" became associated with the rise of Christian fundamentalism. This view opposed any claim for development of separate species through evolutionary processes. The fundamentalist view predominated among Bible believers in that day and still boasts a considerable following. However, even in that early period when the debate flared up, there were "evolutionary creationists" who sought to harmonize the Bible with modern science.

Intelligent Design adherents admit the reality of much

of the science of evolutionary thought but insist that God built into the natural building blocks of life the information, without which there would be no life on earth. ID advocates reject the pure Darwinian theory that a combination of undirected processes – natural selection and random mutations – explains the whole story of species development and consider that it falls short of a biblical account of creation. ID promoters see information in the raw building blocks of life, principally DNA in the genetic code, to have been placed there by the Creator God of the Bible who is thus responsible for all that life is.

Intelligent design advocates are usually not concerned about the controversy between a young and old earth, but accept whatever science says about it. They see evolutionary theory, sometimes referred to as neo-Darwinism, to be an inadequate mechanism to describe what is observed. The debate continues.

Theistic evolution refers to the idea that a creator God set in motion all that life and earth are and let the process develop as it would. It essentially rubber stamps all true science regarding origins. Francis Collins, the scientist who led the effort to map the human genome, is a champion of theistic evolution and a sincere Christian, and with him is a growing number of Christians who also assume his position.

A current focus of the debate

At issue presently is what to do with the Genesis account of creation. Were Adam and Eve real people, or are they representatives of or metaphors for something less personal and historical? Real live people with names and story lines are certainly more interesting and more easily portrayed by a historian or script writer than an account of snail-like changes taking place over long millennia. However, at stake for many is the veracity of the entire Bible with its plan of salvation centered in Jesus Christ. If the Bible is wrong about one, what about the other?

The young or oldish earth creationists face the most crucial dilemma, since they depend on a literalistic rendering of the biblical accounts. For them there must be a real Adam, a real Eve, and so on.

It might be argued that a literal Adam and Eve is necessary for there to be a Fall, the remedy for which is blood atonement brought by the One who bruises the head of the serpent (see Genesis 3). I will leave this issue alone, since my view is that one is independent of the other. Life experience reveals the essential flaw, or evil, at the core of humanity. We need not have an Adam and Eve, a serpent/devil, all in a Garden of Eden, for it to be plain that humankind is lost and depraved.

At the base of the debate is perhaps a fear that somehow contemporary science is an enemy and that specifically evolutionary, godless thought must be challenged at every turn. Let me pose some pertinent questions: Is the debate a distraction? Are we spinning our wheels here and ignoring the simple proclamation of the evangelical gospel? I am reminded that I was a convinced believer in evolution immediately prior to my conversion, and that over four decades of pastoral ministry most of those whom I have seen profess faith in Christ were very much like me. Additionally, must a person hold one scientific concept or another in order to be a Christian? Some say yes and some say no, which is for me the key issue.

Views Christians hold

So then, some Christians hold to a young earth creation with Noah's flood figuring prominently in the scheme. There are older earth creationists who have decided to admit some science unearthed by the archaeologists and geneticists.

Very well and good.

Then there are those who opt for intelligent design, perhaps straddling the fence, and it makes for some fascinating reading, especially considering examples of what is termed "irreducibly complex" organic systems. Here is a safer haven for some who value evolutionary science and want to be what they would consider biblically faithful. Very well and good.

There are also a growing number of those who embrace theistic evolution. They might see the story of Adam and Eve as told in Genesis to be a useful mechanism for an inspired writer to dramatically reveal the circumstances of human beings – made in the image of God but who fall into disobedience and thus can no longer enjoy the fellowship and rest they had with their Creator. We are still doing fine.

An as yet un-named combination view

There are variations on the above schemas also. A fascinating one combines intelligent design and theistic evolution. Here God creates all there is, determines the mechanisms, encodes into all life forms the DNA building blocks, and the millennia march on – but a creature via evolution cannot produce anything close to a being with whom God will have direct fellowship. So then, God steps in and creates Adam and Eve who are made in his image and with whom he does have fellowship. At some unknown, but fairly recently time, creatures suddenly appear, not due to evolution, but due to a special act of creation and made to contain the breath of life.

Let me rephrase the as yet un-named combo view: As I see the theory developing – at some point in history, real time history, the Creator stepped in and made man, male and female, in his image. Adam and Eve, real people, not metaphors, a life form who had the capacity not through evolutionary processes, but a specially made capacity, to communicate with God and have fellowship with him and know him in the deepest sense. Evolution could not get the job done.

Typical of God, he did it himself. It is the primal doctrine of predestination, or election – God's deliberate acting. He created a people for himself, and though they strayed from him, he pursued them and made them his own. From Adam and Eve, in direct descent, came Abraham, Isaac, and Jacob. Israel too, the chosen among whom he dwelt, and in time, the Body of Christ, the elect, the called-out ones.

What I mean is that the Bible records the fact that God is the author of all there is, and that Adam and Eve are the fountain head of the elect.

This combo view allows me to retain the creation account and does not force me to worry about young or oldish earth.[2] This view allows me to acknowledge intelligent design and perhaps theistic evolution as well, which I can also embrace, or at least not feel like I have to reject.

A restatement

Adam and Eve, not evolved but specially made in the image of God, were perhaps even given life in a time frame endorsed by either old earth or younger earth creationists. This preserves a Fall and thus a need for the atonement. I can take the New Testament material about Adam face on and not have to alter it, and neither way would bother me much, because I see this as ultimately a fringe issue.

Such a combination view allows me to fit in rather harmoniously the material found in the early chapters of Genesis that have troubled me over the years. Let me list them:

1) Where did Cain get his wife (see Genesis 4:17)? One would think, taking the Genesis account literally, that only

---

[2] Personally I opt for an old earth, say 13.8 billion years old, but for me the issue is a fringe one and essentially irrelevant.

Adam, Eve, and Cain were alive on the planet. Adjusting upwards the numbers of years these people lived helps but does not solve the problem.

2) The advanced state of husbandry and agriculture necessarily present for Cain to have a garden and Able to have his flock (see Genesis 4:2) is generally understood to have required considerable millennia for our ancestors to master such delicate and complex processes.

3) How was it that the passing of time – consider Methuselah's 969 years in Genesis 5:27 – could be so carefully calculated? Historically, this has been problematic and likely was something that was not arrived at in a hurry.

4) Cain's son Enoch built a city (Genesis 4:17) extremely early on. It puzzles us, knowing the skills required, even if the walls were made of mud.

5) Jubal, the brother of Jabal, played the lyre and pipe (see Genesis 4:21). Wow. Imagine all the human tool-making skills that would have developed prior to something as complicated as musical instruments to be created.

6) Tubal-cain, the great grandson of Jabal "was the forger of all instruments of bronze and iron" (Genesis 4:22). Metallurgy is a rather recent skill comparatively.

There is more, but the point is, I cannot help but think that there must have been considerable cultural and technical knowledge obtained over very lengthy time periods undergirding the activities of these men. No matter, the combo allows for such and retains, at face value, at least from my point of view, the essential biblical truths.

Adam and Eve inherited a great deal of what had been around for a long period of time; they were thrust into a world, that world referred to as "east of Eden," inhabited by other creatures just like themselves but not made in the image of God. (Look below for a discussion of the "sons of God" and "the daughters of God," and look above for the discussion of Cain and his wife.)

Another piece of the puzzle considered

The Books of Moses have a number of interesting stories embedded in them, one of which is found in Genesis 6:1-4. In this particular story may be a clue to the existence of a larger population on the planet that the six instances mentioned above also suggest.

Moses speaks of "the sons of God," "the daughters of man," and the Nephilim or Giants. Though commentators differ as to who was who and what kind of relationships existed between them, one thing is certain: there are two or maybe three different groupings of people to which the writer refers. Some have theorized that the Nephilim were the product of the sons of God taking the daughters of man as wives. Was there intermarriage between the descendants of Seth, God's called-out ones, and those humans who may have occupied the planet for long centuries? The "combo theory" not only allows it but provides a perfect scenario for it actually occurring.

And finally

A tempest in a tea-pot? A lot to do about nothing? A battle that will not be won? A distraction from Christian essentials? A demonic red herring placed in front of the narrow gate? Factioning? Dissensions? All of the above? I opt for this last one. But now for your decision: a title for this essay. I think I know the one I like best. How about you?

Thirty-Two

The Key to Reformed Theology

T he purpose of this essay is to examine the impact of election on the doctrine of salvation. In order to do this it will be necessary to briefly examine some basic views.

Original Sin, Guilt, Infant Baptism, and Covenant Theology.

Classical Calvinism has embedded in it the doctrine of the imputation of sin, meaning that guilt is passed from the parent to the child at conception or at birth, a concept stemming from Augustine and John Calvin. It is characteristic of those who espouse a Reformed theology, as I do, to accept that all people are born with a fallen nature as a result of the sin of Adam and are absolutely inclined toward evil to the point that "all have sinned." The question then is, Are human beings guilty and thus condemned on account of Adam's sin or their own?

However, an additional insistence arises in some Reformed circles that a true Calvinist must hold to a Covenant theology that, in part, defends infant baptism as an event which makes infants and children safe in salvation through that baptism. The practice is usually likened to or is an extension of the command in the Law of Moses that circumcision of the male child be conducted on the eighth day after birth, which act made that child a part of the covenantal community of Israel. This looks to me as tantamount to a separate means of salvation and therefore at least a partial negation of the all encompassing doctrine of the sovereign electing of God.

Typically, those in the Reformed camp embrace two covenants – the covenant of works and the covenant of grace – both of which I maintain. But it is more complicated than that, and when the discussion is done, the conclusion emerges for many that the event of baptism of infants, young children, or even adults establishes the covenant of grace, a covenant between the baptized person and God. Does this do justice to the biblical concept of baptism?

The issue is: How does God save? Is it by means of the baptism of an infant or child? Is it dependent on a covenant relationship with God through the family and/or church? Or is salvation based on election alone?

The Doctrine of Election Stated

Foreknowledge, predestination, election, calling, justification, and glorification are the work of God *and are the terms that describe our salvation.*

> For those whom he foreknew he also predestined to be conformed to the image of his Son, in order that he might be the firstborn among many brothers. And those whom he predestined he also called, and those whom he called he also justified, and those whom he justified he also glorified. Romans 8:29-30

Though the word elect or election is not found specifically in this passage describing the sovereign work of God, the definition of election is the perfect and unifying concept which sums it all up.

From the Hebrew Old Testament *baw-khir* is the transliterated form for the word that is translated as choose, chosen one, or elect. Isaiah used the term in 42:1, 45:4, 65:9, and 65:22 to describe Israel. Israel was selected by God to be His own people; the people themselves did not choose God.

From the Greek New Testament, *eklektos* and *ekloge* are the transliterated forms for the words that are translated as choose, elect, select, or choice. Jesus used eklektos in Matthew 24:22, 24:24, and 24:31; and also in Mark 13:20, 13:22, and 13: 27; then in Luke 18:7 – all in reference to those whom God had chosen.

Paul used the terms in Romans 8:33, Colossians 3:12, 1 Thessalonians 1:4, 1 Timothy 5:21, 2 Timothy 2:10, and Titus 1:1. Peter used the terms in 1 Peter 1:2 and 6, 1 Peter 5:13, and 2 Peter 1:10. John used one of the terms in 2 John 1 and 13.

Election is without question how it is that God calls us to Himself – His foreknowing, predestinating, calling, justifying, and glorifying – all under the grand and large umbrella of election.

Baptism in the New Testament

What then of baptism? It is unquestionably the pattern for new believers in the New Testament to be baptized in water following their conversion, often immediately thereafter. Though no mention of water baptism is mentioned in the missionary work in Cyprus, Antioch of Pisidia, Iconium, Derbe, Lystra, Thessalonica, Berea, or Athens, it is explicitly stated that new converts were baptized in these passages in the Book of Acts: 2:37-41, 8:12, 8:36-38, 9:17-19, 10:44-48, 16:14-15, 16:30-34, 18:8, and 19:1-6. In order then, in

Acts 2:37-41--the new converts on the Day of Pentecost, following Peter's sermon, were baptized. In Acts 8:12—those saved under the ministry of Philip were baptized, as was the Ethiopian Eunuch in Acts 8:36-38. Then Paul was baptized after his conversion in Acts 9:17-19. Cornelius was baptized following his conversion in Acts 10:44-48, as was Lydia and her household as recounted in Acts 16:14-15. The Philippian jailer and his household were baptized in Acts 16:30-34. In Acts 18:8 Crispus and household were baptized upon their conversion, as were the Ephesian converts Paul ministered to in Acts 19:1-6.

Baptism for Households / Baptism for Believers

There are three instances in Acts where "households" were baptized. One – Lydia's (Acts 16:15); two – the Philippian jailer's (Acts 16:33); and three – Crispus' (Acts 18:8). Lydia, the Philippian jailer, and Crispus could have had servants and others present in their households, which would have been common in that era. Whether there were small children in those households is unknown, and so it is not reasonable to base something as critical as baptism, let alone salvation, on silence or conjecture.

"Believer's baptism" or "credo baptism" are terms used by Baptists and many others to describe the baptisms in the New Testament. The Greek word for baptize means to plunge under, dunk, place into the environment of water, immerse, and so on. Many prefer the term immersion, because it more clearly symbolizes the death, burial, and resurrection of Jesus.[1]

Jesus himself was baptized in water by John the Baptist;

---

[1] Proponents of believer's baptism, however, have been known to pour water on the head or sprinkle water on the head when sufficient water is not available or somehow impossible to apply (the proper mode of baptism not being the concern of this essay).

Jesus' disciples, during the course of Jesus' own ministry, performed baptisms as well (see John 4:1-2). Jesus clearly commanded that His disciples baptize new believers (Matthew 28:16-20). Paul baptized, though he made it clear that "Christ did not send me to baptize but to preach the gospel, and not with words of eloquent wisdom, lest the cross of Christ be emptied of its power" (1 Corinthians 1:17). It is evident that Paul did not think that baptizing was a saving event.

Baptism: a Confession of Faith

Water baptism is important for a number of reasons, all solidly biblical, but the act itself is not a saving one. What counts is God's election. Baptism, which follows conversion, fulfills the command of Jesus to baptize, a command He made to His Church. His command to new believers to be baptized provides for a public confession of faith in Christ, which is actually a testimony to the Gospel and an identification of the baptized person as belonging to Christ and His Church. Baptism in the New Testament is not an insignificant detail.

Church history on the issue of baptism

This limited view of baptism has not been, nor is today, the unanimous conclusion of the visible church. In the Creed of the Council of Constantinople of 381, commonly called the Nicene Creed, is the statement, "We acknowledge one baptism for the forgiveness of sins."

Constantine himself, who convened the initial council of Nicaea in A.D.325, refused to be baptized until he knew he was close to death, since the concept had already taken root in the fourth century church that baptism washed away sin, but only sins previously committed.

Beginning somewhere in the late second or early third century, baptism took on saving properties in the thinking of church leaders. The Apostolic Fathers had previously held closely to the New Testament views that baptism was something someone submitted to following conversion and which served as a means of obeying the commands of Jesus to be baptized. It was considered a way to declare that Jesus was Lord and functioned as a public testimony of identification with Jesus and the Christian community, among other things. However, the Church Fathers, that group of leading Christians who followed in time after the Apostolic Fathers, began to depart from their predecessors and elevated baptism to a place foreign to the views of the New Testament writers.

The earliest clear evidence that the Church had begun to baptize infants is found in the writings of Origen (A.D. 185-254): "Every soul that is born into flesh is soiled by the filth of wickedness and sin. In the Church, baptism is given for the remission of sins, and, according to the usage of the Church, baptism is given even to infants" (from a sermon based on Leviticus 8:3). In Origen, the Greek dualistic notion of a separate existence, even pre-existence, of a soul is evident. It is apparent then that the concept of baptism's efficacy for washing away sin was held by some in the early third century.

Biblical Support?

The Church Fathers did find some biblical support for infant baptism. Two New Testament passages at first reading seem to indicate that baptism is a saving event. Peter, in the Jerusalem Pentecost sermon said, "Repent and be baptized every one of you in the name of Jesus Christ for the forgiveness of your sins, and you will receive the gift of the Holy Spirit" (Acts 2:38). But then again, in Peter's second sermon in Jerusalem, this one delivered in Solomon's Portico in the Temple, he said, "Repent therefore, and turn again, that your sins may be blotted out" (Acts 3:19). Actually, Peter meant the same in both places, since many Jews in that era, especially those who were expecting the arrival of the Messiah, equated repentance with baptism: to demonstrate repentance one would be publicly baptized. And repentance meant to change one's mind about the Messiah and who He was, as there were a number of competing ideas abroad.

Then in 1 Peter 3:21 we read, "Baptism, which corresponds to this, now saves you, not as a removal of dirt from the body but as an appeal to God for a good conscience, through the resurrection of Jesus Christ." Peter's reference is to Noah and his family saved from judgment by means of the flood waters by being in the ark. Baptism is a vivid portrayal of being delivered from judgment, a dramatic means of picturing the death, burial, and resurrection of Jesus. Jesus is like the ark of salvation that carried Noah safely through the threatening storm of God's wrath. And Peter makes it clear that baptism is not a cleansing from sin event but is rather an appeal to God for a good or clear conscience. Baptism is important but not saving, and it is grounded in the death and resurrection of Christ.

From Whence Comes Our Guilt?

Many point to Psalm 51:5 and appeal to David's lament as support to insist that a person is born guilty, which for some opens the door to infant baptism and more importantly, to diminishing the doctrine of election: "Behold, I was brought forth in iniquity, and in sin did my mother conceive me."

Psalm 51 is one of David's penitential songs, this one written by the guilt-stricken king after the prophet Nathan confronted him over his adultery with Bathsheba and the murder of her husband, Uriah. David declares his own sinfulness and does not intend to blame his mother for his own failure, much less to theologize that he was condemned while in the womb. Does the passage teach guilt from conception or birth? Or is it an expression of grief over sin and the realization of being utterly sinful as far back as memories or imaginings could go?

The Psalm is a song; it is poetry, not a statement of doctrine. It does agree with Jeremiah 17:9, "The heart is deceitful above all things and desperately sick." Yet it is a reach too far to suggest that the verse teaches guilt at conception or birth.

Next let us consider Paul's statements in Romans 5, verses 12 to 21:

> Therefore, just as sin came into the world through one man, and death through sin, and so death spread to all men because all sinned – for sin indeed was in the world before the law was given, but sin is not counted where there is no law. Yet death reigned from Adam to Moses, even over those whose sinning was not like the transgression of Adam, who was a type of the one who was to come.
>
> But the free gift is not like the trespass. For if many died through one man's trespass, much more have the grace of God and the free gift by the grace of that one man Jesus Christ abounded for many. And the free gift is not like the result of that one man's sin. For the judgment following one trespass brought condemnation, but the free gift following many trespasses brought justification. For if, because of one man's trespass, death reigned through that one man, much more will those who receive the abundance of grace and the free gift of righteousness reign in life through the one man Jesus Christ.

Therefore, as one trespass led to condemnation for all men, so one act of righteousness leads to justification and life for all men. For as by one man's disobedience the many were made sinners, so by the one man's obedience the many will be made righteous. Now the law came in to increase the trespass, but where sin increased, grace abounded all the more, so that, as sin reigned in death, grace also might reign through righteousness leading to eternal life through Jesus Christ our Lord.

Does Paul teach that guilt is present from conception, or for that matter, from birth? No, in my view, he does not. Paul is stressing that sin and death had their entry into the human family through Adam. Adam sinned, and the door was opened – nothing will be the same, until the future arrival of heaven and the kingdom of God.

What Paul does teach is that, through Adam's law-breaking, death and sin entered into the world, and death spread to all humans as a result. The meaning of "death" here is crucial. Is it physical death, or is it separation from the fellowship Adam had enjoyed with his Maker prior to the rebellion or Fall? Satan told Eve that there would be no death, contradicting what God had said (see Genesis 2:16 and 3:1-4). Indeed, after their sin Adam and Eve did not physically die; rather they were driven from God's presence and sent East of Eden. Salvation and eternal life is the re-entry into God's presence, as Revelation chapters 21 and 22 so beautifully describe. Once again, God and man will be "face to face" (Revelation 22:4). Ever since Adam, we have been separated from God because of our sin. We can only have fellowship with God and be reconciled to Him through the person and work of our Lord Jesus Christ.

It is essential to note that Paul said directly that "death

spread to all men because *all sinned*." He had the perfect opportunity to state that all the guilt of all the people who would be Adam's descendents (all humans) proceeded from Adam. Instead he repeated what he had made clear in Romans 3:23: "For *all have sinned* and fall short of the glory of God."

Guilt is the focus of the discussion, so the question is whether people are condemned for Adam's sin or for their own. At some point in early Church history, due to the influences of pagan Greek myths, it was decided that is was Adam's sin that condemns us. It was only a natural progression, then, to desire some mechanism to deal with that problem, especially for infants or children who die. Infant baptism was the solution and continues to be so for large numbers of Christians. From my understanding of things, however, election is the better answer.

The Limitations of Basing Doctrine on Scant Evidence

Experience has taught me that systems, however logical and developed by great theologians, are helpful and necessary, but they may well be flawed at points, as our fallen nature would predict. I prefer to see really large and crucial theological positions clearly revealed in the Old Testament, and I am most comfortable when they are spelled out or loudly hinted at in the Torah, the Prophets, and the Writings – all three. Then, in addition, I want to see them clearly, explicitly, in the Gospels, meaning in the mouth of Jesus. Finally, core doctrine should be evident in the writings of the earliest Church, meaning clearly presented in the Book of Acts or in the letters of Paul, Peter, John, James, or Jude. The basics of the doctrine of salvation cannot be anchored on interpretations of a couple of passages that allow for varying understandings.

Serious Debate Abounds

Sometimes I wonder about the intramural debates among those of us who embrace the Doctrines of Grace. It is not enough for some to affirm inability and completely reject Pelagianism or its cousin, semi-Pelagianism.[2] Instead, a quasi-sectarian attitude seems to be present.

Some insist that Calvin, along with Augustine, taught that condemnation of the individual is present at birth, if not from conception, and is why infant baptism is necessary. For them, rejection of the bed rock view of original sin, that the first sin resulted in guilt and condemnation of all human beings, actually amounts to a rejection of Reformed Theology in general.[3]

Others say that every individual – each child of Adam and Eve – is fallen, sinful, depraved, twisted, and bent on evil, but they simultaneously say that condemnation is the result of personal sin and not the sin of Adam.

Small point? No, it is at the heart of the intramural debate, and the erupting controversy obscures the discovery of the biblical Doctrines of Grace for those who are emerging from long held Arminian points of view.

---

2 Pelagianism: belief that salvation lies within the capacity of a person. Semi-Pelagianism: salvation depends on a cooperation of God and man, a synergy, but man can reject the grace of God by not believing, so the man is ultimately in control. The Doctrines of Grace at least state that a person can in no way determine his or her eternal destination, but that salvation is all of God.

3 Original sin may refer to (1) the very first sin—that of Adam and Eve; or (2) the condemning impact of that first sin upon the offspring of Adam and Eve. My contention is that every person inherits a sinful nature and is steadfastly bent toward evil. Condemnation, and therefore the need for salvation, comes from the individual act of sin, which each living person will commit.

Election: the final word

My anchor is the doctrine of election. Whether one is committed to infant baptism or not, whether one is convinced that every person is condemned for Adam's or their own disobedience, or whatever view about lostness one might have, election overcomes them all. Augustinianism, Calvinism, Lutheranism, or ___ism, the whole of the matter is the electing grace of God. Because of God's electing, anything a human being does amounts to nothing in terms of absolute salvation. Discipleship, obedience, and the full range of all of that contributes to sanctification are other issues entirely.

The point is not whether a person is condemned from conception or birth, based on the inheritance of a fallen and corrupt nature, or whether he will join all humanity in the ranks of "all have sinned and fall short of the glory of God." The point is that all are sinners and in need of grace. My view, and the point of this essay, is that the saving mercy and grace of God comes through election only. Everything and anything else practiced by churches and individuals – ceremonies, sacraments, and rituals – are ultimately beside the point. Every form of baptism is of no avail when it comes to salvation. A miscarriage, a still birth, an abortion, or some other horrifying circumstance will not nullify or deter saving grace – election trumps all.

Therefore, when the worry and the question arises, Can the unbaptized be saved?, the answer, in light of election, is yes, and a resounding YES!

Thirty-Three

Male/Female: The Nature of God

So God created man in his own image, in the image of God he created him; male and female he created them (Genesis 1:27).

Can it be deduced from Genesis 1:27 that God in his very being and essence is both male and female?

The answer to this question might be approached by asking two other questions: Is the male alone the image of God? Is the female alone the image of God?

The history of interpretation on this issue is long and complicated, not to mention conflicting, yet arriving at an interpretation will be fundamental to maintaining basic biblical theology. The following interpretive statements focus on the issues of homosexuality and the potential making of idols.

The pronouns used for God in all but some of the newer translations are "he," "him," and "his." This is because the Bible authors used these masculine pronouns consistently to refer to the Creator God, preferring clarity and simplicity. Bible authors could have chosen to use feminine pronouns but did not. Were the reasons dictated by cultural norms, accepted literary devices, doctrinal necessities, or the result of the influence of the Holy Spirit on the inspired writers? Since the issue is not directly taken up in holy writ, we cannot be dogmatically sure, but many of us would lean toward the last possibility. If so, why then does God choose to refer to himself the way he does?

My view is that essential core doctrines are the determining factor.

One such doctrine has to do with marriage. **One male with one female** is a fundamental requirement for marriage, since procreation is central to the purpose of God, as seen in Genesis 1:28: "And God blessed them. And God said to them, 'Be fruitful and multiply.'" Neither two males nor two females can procreate. This truth remains, despite so-called medical advances and capabilities that provide a myriad of new options for conception.[1] Only the union in marriage between a man and a woman reflects the nature of God. God is in essence a unit – an *echad* in the Hebrew – male and female according to Genesis 1:27. Marriage between a man and a woman is a picture of God. A man leaves his father and his mother and holds fast to his wife, and they then become one flesh (see Genesis 2:24). The "one" is *echad*, a unit of two combined so as not to be divided. Thus, divorce is a violation of the purpose of God but became necessary due to our hardness of heart and general sinfulness. God, however, will not be divided, and to do so in any of the myriad of ways humans have designed and attempted is idol-making.

Two males and two females cannot, in fact, be married in the economy of God. Human tampering with this can only result in idolatry. The offspring of Adam and Eve will do what

---

[1] New techniques for conception, in my view, are a blessing to those who are not able to conceive otherwise. And, I do not view human sexuality to be for procreation alone; sex is a glue, a bond, that humans need and also a way to express love in a deep and personal way.

they will do, but it is meaningless huffing and puffing when weighed in the courts of heaven. Homosexuality, however refined and made culturally proper, cannot ever reflect the original creation or the *echad* of God. It is therefore a rejection of God and gross idol-making.

Finally, the centrality of the unity intended in creation of male and female as it reflects the fundamental essence and being of God also points to and is integral to the recreation, the marriage of Christ and his bride, the Church. Christ will come for his bride. There will be a marriage supper. There will be a uniting for eternity with no divorce possible (see Revelation 21).

Part of the creation is the union of a male and a female; the recreation is the uniting of Christ the male and His Church the female. The bride and the bridegroom is the eternal *echad* and is the ultimate intent of the creator God who is both male and female at once.

Thirty-Four

Walking, Talking, and Eating with Jesus

(This essay is based on Luke 24:13-35)

Some evangelical Christians are anxious to walk with God and hungry to talk with God, even hoping he would stop by and eat a meal with them.

The desire to experience God in a direct and concrete way is impacting Christians all over the world, and it seems especially so in the United States. Indeed, the Creator of the universe is said, in our present day, to be manifesting himself directly to those who desire a close encounter with him.

Many of those claiming to have personal contact with God himself were converted during the Jesus People Movement of the late 1960s and early 1970s. Their desire for this is understandable, since during that great outpouring of the Holy Spirit, God was moving powerfully among us. They saw that great outpouring diminish, as it always does when God brings an awakening to its close, and they miss it.

Many religious traditions, both inside and outside the Christian Church, have pursued means of contact with God that are questionable, even unbiblical. But in our Bible is a story which reveals how God may be sought and found, even be experienced in a healthy and biblically sanctioned way.

Two disciples who walked, talked, and ate with Jesus

At some time during the first Easter Sunday, on the narrow dirt path that ran seven miles from Jerusalem to Emmaus, two discouraged disciples of Jesus met a stranger who seemingly just happened along.[1] At two miles an hour average, which is likely a good guess at their walking speed, the conversation could have lasted several hours.

The stranger approached the two as they were discussing events that had recently taken place in Jerusalem and wanted to know what the two had been talking about. One of them, Cleopas, assuming the stranger had also been in Jerusalem and somewhat surprised at the question, wondered aloud how this man could be the only who did not know what had happened. Not irritated by the question, the stranger seemed to simply want to know more.

Both disciples related how Jesus of Nazareth, a man who was a mighty prophet, had been rejected by the religious leaders and finally put to death on a cross. This event had crushed their hopes, since they thought Jesus was the long awaited Messiah of Israel.

But that was not all. They told of some women who were part of their company who had been, that very morning, to the tomb where Jesus' body had been placed three days earlier. They could not find his body, but had seen a vision of angels who told them Jesus was alive. Not only that, but upon investigation by other men of the group, the women's claim that there was no body in the tomb was verified. But the men did not see Jesus himself.

The stranger listened to the account, and then told them

---

[1] The name of one of the disciples is Cleopas, and the other is unnamed. Some scholars have suggested that the unnamed person was the wife of Cleopas.

how slow of heart they were not to believe all that the prophets had said. In fact, he pointed out that the Messiah, of necessity, must suffer and then enter into his glory, that is, die and then be raised from the dead. And then, most incredibly, "beginning with Moses and all the Prophets, he interpreted to them in all the Scriptures the things concerning himself."[2]

The two most fortunate disciples had been walking and talking with God the Son, the resurrected Christ, in person. How we wish we could have been there!

At Emmaus

Having reached their destinations, Cleopas and his companion persuaded the very captivating and now less strange companion to accompany them home and stay with them, since the daylight was fading away.

At the dinner table, their new friend took bread, said a traditional Jewish blessing thanking the King of the universe for providing for them, then broke it in pieces and gave some to each. At once the men recognized who this man was. Though not of the twelve apostles, they nonetheless had been with Jesus when he had broken bread before, and now there could be no question about it. Jesus was there with them, eating a meal. He had been talking with them, walking with them, and now eating with them.

Then the Lord was gone, vanished! Just like that, without the record of a good bye. No matter, they simply said to each to other, "Did not our hearts burn within us while he talked to us on the road, while he opened to us the Scriptures?" Their hearts burned within them, which is precisely what we want, too.

---

2   Luke fast forwards here in Luke 24:27 when he uses the phrase, "concerning himself" as Jesus would not be know other than as a stranger until later in the story, specifically verse 31.

Back to Jerusalem

Now, the reasons for the trip to Emmaus no longer mattered to them, so back to Jerusalem they went, because they had proof positive that Jesus was alive. Upon their arrival in the city, perhaps finding Peter and the rest hiding in the same Upper Room where they had celebrated Passover together just a few days earlier, they made it clear that they had recognized Jesus during the "breaking of the bread."

The Biblical Model

Based on the story "On the Road to Emmaus" in Luke 24:13-35, we have a model of walking, talking, and eating with Jesus in a way that provides a biblical encounter and experience of God.

First, we see the "burning of the hearts" when Jesus interpreted the Scriptures for them. Jesus did the one thing that would prove to be so valuable to the two disciples: he opened up the Word of God to them. Jesus is present in his Word. If we desire to walk, talk, and eat with Jesus, we go to his Word. And the preachers and teachers whom God raises up will do that very same thing – go to the Scripture and find Jesus there and give it out to his disciples.

Second, we see that Cleopas and friend recognized Jesus when he broke bread with them. Maybe it was a re-enactment of the Passover, or at least a part of it, or perhaps the simple giving out of a loaf of bread, but there it was. They were in the presence of Jesus as they broke the bread, and so may we be. Remember the words "Do this in remembrance of me."[3] We know from Acts 2:42, with its description of the core elements of the early Christian community, how important the breaking of the bread was: "And they devoted themselves to the apostles' teaching and fellowship to the breaking of

---

3 Luke 22:19.

bread and the prayers."[4] When we desire to walk, talk, and eat with Jesus, we know that in the Scripture, that is both testaments of our wonderful Bible, we will meet Jesus. Likewise, we will see Jesus, recognize Jesus, be with Jesus, and eat with Jesus in the breaking of the bread.

The four activities that Luke describes in Acts 2:42 as being central to early Christian experience and worship all may bring us into the presence of God. We will find Jesus in hearing the Scripture expounded and preached. We will encounter Jesus in the communion of fellowship, as Christian brothers and sisters are part of the household of God, the Body of Christ. We will have Jesus' presence in the breaking of bread. Perhaps the purest experience of God with us is in our prayers – entering boldly into the presence of God, whether alone or in a congregation. These four parts of a decidedly biblical model are given to us that we might experience the glorified Christ.

Our Christianity is intensely mystical and spiritual; we need not go beyond the biblical model into realms that are questionable, maybe even dangerous. We do not have to wander away from normal, healthy Christian and Scriptural forms to encounter the living God.

---

4 Whether "breaking of bread" was a standalone ritual or a segment of a larger meal, perhaps the agape feast, it is not clear from the context. Nevertheless, however it was, Jesus may be found there.

Other Books by Kent Philpott

The Soul Journey: How Shamanism, Santería, Wicca, and Charisma are Connected

If the Devil Wrote a Bible

Memoirs of a Jesus Freak

Awakenings in America and the Jesus People Movement

How Christians Cast Out Demons Today

A Matter of Life and Death: Understanding True and False Conversion

Are You Being Duped?

Why I Am a Christian

For Pastors of Small Churches

How to Care for Your Pastor

EVP

Earthen Vessel Publishing
Visit www.evpbooks.com

www.ingramcontent.com/pod-product-compliance
Lightning Source LLC
LaVergne TN
LVHW051116080426
835510LV00018B/2076